For Ambassador
Geoffrey Pyatt
With love and high esteem
☩Archbishop Demetrios of America
New York
June 23, 2017

Archbishop Demetrios of America

Primate of the Greek Orthodox Church in America
Exarch of the Ecumenical Patriarchate

Ways of the Lord

Perspectives on Sharing the Gospel of Christ

Πᾶσαι αἱ ὁδοὶ Κυρίου ἔλεος καὶ ἀλήθεια

(Ψαλμός 24.10, Psalm 25:10)

Greek Orthodox Archdiocese of America
New York
2010

Greek Orthodox Archdiocese of America
8 East 79th Street, New York, NY 10075

©2010 by the Greek Orthodox Archdiocese of America

ISBN 1-58438-031-4

All Rights Reserved
Printed in the United States of America

*This book is dedicated to
His All Holiness Ecumenical Patriarch Bartholomew,
the champion of panorthodox unity,
interreligious and intercultural dialogue,
and recognition of the sanctity of the environment
as creation of God*

Table of Contents

Prologue — vii

Ageless Traditions in a New Millennium
35th Clergy-Laity Congress Keynote
Philadelphia, PA - July 3, 2000 — 1

Offering Our Orthodox Faith to Contemporary America
36th Clergy-Laity Congress Keynote
Los Angeles, CA - July 1, 2002 — 19

Building Communities of Faith and Love: Orthodox Parishes in Worship and Ministry
37th Clergy-Laity Congress Keynote
New York, NY - July 26, 2004 — 37

Sharing the Truth of the Gospel and the Love of Christ
38th Clergy-Laity Congress Keynote
Nashville, TN - July 17, 2006 — 53

Gather My People to My Home
39th Clergy-Laity Congress Keynote
Washington, DC - July 14, 2008 — 69

Universal Values of Religions
Address to Symposium on Universal Values
Athens, Greece - May 26, 2004 — 89

A Christian Spirituality of Peace and
Justice in a Violent World
    Conference on Violence and Spirituality
    Brookline, MA - October 27, 2005   **103**

A Free Society Founded on Truth:
Truth Making People Free
    Istanbul, Turkey - October 20-21, 2005   **117**

The Dynamics of the Orthodox Faith
in Contemporary America
    Orthodoxy in America Lecture Series
    Fordham University - February 4, 2004   **131**

The Ecumenical Patriarchate and its
Ministry of Reconciliation
    Sacred Heart University - November 9, 2005   **155**

Some Suggestions for Cultivating
Interreligious Dialogue
    Fairfield University - November 14, 2007   **172**

Τά 'Ανθρώπινα 'Αδιέξοδα καί
οἱ Πατέρες τῆς 'Εκκλησίας
    Πανεπιστήμιον Κύπρου - 26 Ἰανουαρίου 2006   **185**

Human Impasses and the Church Fathers
    University of Cyprus - January 26, 2006   **209**

Index   **233**

Prologue

The Gospel of Jesus Christ is by its very nature a living and dynamic reality, a reality to be shared by many, if not by all human beings. The Gospel as sacred text and as a vital presence experienced by communities or by individuals cannot be in a status of immobility, stagnation or inertia. Also, it cannot be kept as the exclusive and unshared ownership of the ones who have been blessed to have received it. The permanent, absolute, and uncompromising condition of the Gospel of Jesus Christ is the condition of transmitting it, of sharing it, of making it the precious property of more and more people.

Sharing the Gospel with those who do not know it can be at times an uncomplicated task as we know from the long history of Christianity. Frequently, however, and especially in our days, the very same task seems to require more elaborate, methodical and sophisticated approaches. The texts presented in this book constitute an humble effort to contribute to such a task, which is the sacred but also demanding work of sharing the Gospel with the people of today; hence, the subtitle of the book "Perspectives on Sharing the Gospel of Christ".

The perspectives are presented in the forms of keynotes, lectures, addresses, and speeches given on various occasions in the last few years. In spite of their differentiated content, all of them in essence aim at facilitating, in one way or another, the task of sharing the Gospel, of increasing its availability to larger numbers of people. It is imperative that promising perspectives must be presented effectively, plans and projects must be worked out, mindful of what the One who is the center of the Gospel said, *Without me you can do nothing* (John 15:5). This is why the title of the present book is *Ways of the Lord*. He gave to us the Gospel. He is the Gospel. Ultimately, He knows and He can teach us ways to share the Gospel with everyone, be it our next door neighbor or persons living in another country or even on another continent. We know well that *all the ways of the Lord are mercy and truth* (Psalm 24:10). In the final analysis, mercy and truth are the real perspectives and effective methods of sharing the Gospel of Christ.

This book is not an individual product. It incorporates, in many of its parts, the precious experience of our dynamic Communities of the Greek Orthodox Archdiocese of America, and the amazing faith witness of our Ecumenical Patriarchate of Constantinople. On the technical side, the book is the product of significant labor by many people involving transcriptions, editing and preparation of the final manuscript for publication. To all of them I express my deep gratitude and my warmest wishes for abundant blessings from the Giver and Lord of the Gospel. My fervent prayers accompany also all the people who will be kind enough to read this book.

†DEMETRIOS
Archbishop of America
Pascha 2010 - New York

Ways of the Lord

Perspectives on Sharing the Gospel of Christ

Ageless Traditions in a New Millennium

35th Clergy-Laity Congress Keynote Address

Philadelphia, Pennsylvania
July 3, 2000

A. The Three Tasks

1. Introduction

Blessing and glory and wisdom and thanksgiving and honor and power and might be to our God forever and ever. Amen (Revelation 7:12).

This beautiful biblical hymn of the book of the Revelation of John constituted my opening statement at the Enthronement ceremony on September 18, 1999, in the Holy Trinity Cathedral of New York.

Today, nine months later here in Philadelphia at the 35th Clergy-Laity Congress of the Holy Greek Orthodox Archdiocese of America, I am starting again with the very same hymn: *Blessing and glory and wisdom and thanksgiving and honor and power and might be to our God forever and ever. Amen.* But this time, my intense feelings of fervent worship and adoration to God are accompanied by an overwhelming sense of gratitude and awe for the precious and unique experience of living for the past nine months with you, of working with you, of serving you, of worshipping with you, of sharing with you the joys and the pains of the work of God here in America.

During those nine months of intense work I have had the constant and warm support of His All Holiness the Ecumenical Patriarch Bartholomew and the Holy and Sacred Synod of the Ecumenical Patriarchate. I am deeply grateful to them.

I am also filled with thankfulness towards my beloved Brothers, the Metropolitans and Bishops, especially the Hierarchs of our Eparchial Synod. We have enjoyed a genuine, inspiring, and creative brotherly cooperation, particularly during our many meetings. I am also extending my deep thanks to the SCOBA Hierarchs for an excellent cooperation.

What can I say for our pious clergy and for the lay people whom I encountered in my numerous pastoral visitations to the parishes or in many other occasions! I can but only repeat what Saint Paul said to the Corinthians: *I give thanks to God always for you for the grace of God which was given to you in Christ Jesus, that in every way you were enriched in Him* (I Corinthians 1:4-5).

The people of the various institutions, administrative bodies and functions of the Archdiocese, however related to it are an integral part of the contents of my gratefulness to God and to the people: the Archdiocesan Council and its Executive Committee, the Archdiocesan Presbyters Council, the Philoptochos, the Archons of our Ecumenical Patriarchate, Hellenic College/Holy Cross, Leadership 100, Saint Basil Academy, Saint Michael's Home, the Hellenic Cultural Center, OCMC, IOCC, Saint

Photios National Shrine, Saint Nicholas Ranch, the National Sisterhood of Presvyteres, the Forum of Church Musicians, the Benefits Committee, and of course, the beloved workers of the Archdiocesan, the Diocesan, and the parish offices. But the list is not complete. And what more shall I say? For time would fail me to tell of all those to whom I am indebted (cf. Hebrews 11:32).

Inundated with gratitude for what we have received and experienced and for the remarkable people that God has raised in this Church, people whom I am meeting every day, we are now here, at our 35th Clergy-Laity Congress. We are here to think and to pray, to discuss and to decide, to plant and to build, in the presence of God and in a spirit of love, unity, respect and dignity.

We have been granted the joy as individuals and as a Greek American Orthodox Community to be able to live at a crucial time, at a historic milestone. There is a significance in the fact that we live in the year 2000, which is a number inviting serious reflection because it is connected to a new century and a new millennium. It is a number that opens up a future which might be a challenging, promising, perhaps threatening, yet enticing future.

How do we face this future? What do we plan for the years to come as a Greek American Orthodox Community? Being a truly blessed and richly gifted ecclesiastical body, where are we moving from the present point of our life?

I should like to suggest that, among others, there are three major tasks, three major objectives in front of us. They constitute the contents of the theme of our 35th Congress: "Ageless Traditions in a New Millennium." These tasks are related to our long history as a Church, to our potential, to our role in this country and to the challenges of the new time span opened to us. They are related to the fact that we are the carriers of extremely precious and ageless traditions which must be strong and decisive agents in the formation of our lives in the new millennium. In essence they are tasks depending on and generated by the fact and substance of our Orthodox faith, if we understand this faith as an alive, dynamic, and creative reality.

2. The Tradition of Faith as Worship and Prayer

The first is the task of living and experiencing faith as worship and prayer. Our Greek Orthodox Church has been a Church known throughout the past twenty centuries for her rich and exquisite liturgical tradition and prayer life. She has been known as a worshipping Church *par excellence*, constantly demonstrating faith as worship, faith as an adoring connector to God via prayer. Hence, our *Ecclesia* has developed a tremendous wealth of differentiated services and prayer opportunities covering all days, all circumstances, all aspects of human life. The worshipping fervor and character of our Church has been strongly and amply presented in the extraordinary development of arts related to the liturgical activities: the architectural masterpieces in building Churches, the superb iconographic achievements, and the amazing productions of the ecclesiastical music, to mention a few.

Here we have an ageless tradition of faith as worship, an intense, full, genuine and spiritual worship, in absolute line with the saying of our Lord: *God is Spirit, and those who worship Him must worship in Spirit and in truth*: Πνεῦμα ὁ Θεός, καὶ τοὺς προσκυνοῦντας αὐτὸν ἐν πνεύματι καὶ ἀληθείᾳ δεῖ προσκυνεῖν (John 4:24). Such a tradition must remain not only highly active, but become increasingly intensified and enhanced in the years ahead. This is a tradition which aims at connecting and, ultimately, at uniting all human beings to God, at creating a constant line of communication between Creator and creatures, between the Heavenly Father and His earthly sons and daughters. This is an ageless tradition of liberating us from the bondage to the material and of presenting us with the freedom of the unlimited vistas of the spiritual world of God.

In view of the rampant technological evolution in the new millennium, in view of increasing stressors interfering with human life, in view of a cruel domination of the secular and the material, the need for constant opening to God is urgent and imperative. A Church which experiences and projects her faith as worship and prayer, which is both intense and alive, will be in a position to offer this liberating opening to the people. Here, we have a bright opportunity in the time ahead of us.

3. The Tradition of Faith as Love

The second major task is the task of experiencing and projecting faith as love in all its possible expressions: love, care, charity, gentleness, *diaconia*. Our Orthodox Church has been a Church of love in its two dimensions or fields: love within the Church among its members, and love spreading outside of the Church and addressed to every human being.

Such multidimensional love, generated by faith in a God who is love, has been a central component of the ageless traditions of the Church. This precise tradition, this characteristic of a loving and caring Church, seems to be definitively needed in the new century, in the new millennium.

The Lord Jesus Christ warned His disciples that at certain times in the future, because wickedness is multiplied, most people's love will grow cold: καὶ διὰ τὸ πληθυνθῆναι τὴν ἀνομίαν ψυγήσεται ἡ ἀγάπη τῶν πολλῶν (Matthew 24:12). True love might become more and more a rarity, replaced by passing emotionalism and coldly calculated relationships. Expressions of kindness might give their place to manipulating techniques. Specialists in public relations and behavioral techniques might be in demand by people motivated by the selfish desire to be served rather than to serve, to dominate and to intimidate rather than to love. Society might gradually become a maze of isolated individuals, a crowd of non-loving, non-connecting persons.

The ageless tradition of faith as love, as a vivid manifestation of Christ's presence among us, becomes an absolute necessity. What oxygen and water are for the preservation and growth of life on earth, love and true unity among people are for the preservation and enhancement of human existence in any given society. We are the carriers of that ageless tradition of faith as love; we are the embodiments of that uniting power. In a new millennium where love and loving connections and commitments among people might diminish, we have a magnificent mission: to show in action that a world without love is a dead world, that a society without care and tender concern for each other is a terrifying monster.

Here is a mission of unheard of proportions and truly salvific consequences: to become the apostles of faith as love, the constant transmitters of the divine message for an unlimited opening to the people, leading to spiritual connectiveness and unity of hearts. You are familiar with the warning: "Attention! Danger! High voltage-live electrical wire! Do not touch!" We as Church must provide society with a different warning: "Attention! No Danger! High power-live wire of love! Please touch! Please connect!" We must, however, have a network of such high power wires of love immediately available. This is our destiny and our mission in the days and years ahead of us.

4. The Tradition of Faith as Truth

The third major task is the task of experiencing faith as truth: as truth about God, about us, about the universe; as truth about life and death, pain and joy; as truth about our destiny, about the meaning of life, about the purpose of life.

Truth on all the above listed areas belongs to the ageless traditions of our Orthodox Faith. The Lord of the Church, Jesus Christ declared: *I am the way and the truth and the life* (John 14:6), thus directly connecting truth to life and action. The same Lord, when He promised His disciples to send them the Holy Spirit, said: *When the Holy Spirit comes, He will guide you into the whole truth* (John 16:13). And in His final prayer He asked the Heavenly Father: *Father, sanctify them* (i.e. the disciples) *in Your truth; Your word is truth* (John 17:17). Truth belongs to the very heart of the Gospel.

This ageless tradition of faith as truth has been constantly operative in our Church. It was this unyielding adherence to a faith based on the truth that led millions of martyrs to die rather than abandon or betray God's truth. It was this unquenchable thirst and passion for the truth which produced the great Fathers and Teachers of the Church. It was the dedication to the tradition of faith as truth, as revealed to humanity by Christ, that caused the amazing work of the Ecumenical Councils which kept that truth integral, inviolable, pure and radiant.

What is the new era before us going to do to the truth—to the truth of God and to the truth in general? Who is going to control the websites and the Internet and the media, and prevent them from becoming constant, increasingly powerful sources for prefabricated misinformation, semi-truths, mixtures of lies, imagination and data? Are the next generations going to experience an eclipse of the truth, a relativization of it and a transformation of the truth into a word-play without significance?

Here again we are called by God to stand firm on the ground of an ageless tradition of our faith which declares that without truth as a central component in life, there is no meaning in life, there is no possibility for real knowledge and cultivation of this divine gift which is our mind, our intellect.

We are being sent by God to be the carriers, the guardians, the transmitters of His truth in the coming years. We have been given the great privilege to radiate faith as truth, to take the torch of an eternal and ageless truth from the hands of the Apostles, the Martyrs, the Saints, the Fathers, the Ecumenical Synods; and to hold it fast in our hands, to march in the dark paths of the world—to march and to illumine, to walk and to plant truth, to run and to generously distribute the truth of God preserved as a priceless, ageless tradition in the life of our Greek Orthodox Church, a tradition related to the substance of our faith, to the educational, teaching, and learning practices of our ecclesial life.

Ultimately, what we have to do is not simply to juxtapose or to oppose truth to falsehood. What we have to do is to oppose faith as truth to chaos, faith as knowledge to messy information, faith as intelligence to confusion of ideas and minds. What we have to do is to be steadfast in projecting the faith which is intertwined with the truth and which guarantees the truth as an absolute given in life.

Three of the most important and vital ageless traditions of our Greek Orthodox heritage seem to be our priorities in the new millennium, in view of the characteristics and the special features of that millennium:

(1) The tradition of faith as worship and prayer, i.e. the tradition of a vibrant, beautiful, all-encompassing liturgical and prayer life that connects with God;

(2) The tradition of faith as love, i.e. a strong, loving, caring, serving attitude, as a lifestyle connecting us to the other people;

(3) And finally, the tradition of faith as truth, i.e. a tradition of adhering, guarding, and promoting the truth of God versus the proliferation of a chaotic misinformation, a predominance of falsehood and an intellectual confusion.

Those are general views and visions for our role as a Greek American Orthodox Church and as individual members of the Greek Orthodox Church in America, as we face the new developments in human history ushered in by the twenty-first century and the third millennium. Let me proceed, however, at this point with some specific applications of the above-presented main tasks.

B. *Special Applications*

1. The Tradition of Faith as Worship and Prayer

For the first task related to the offering on our part of faith as worship in a vibrant liturgical and prayer life, I should like to invite all of us to think about the worshipping conditions of the specific community in which each one lives.

a) How is our Sunday liturgy and its attendance?

b) How much liturgical and prayer life do we have as a community, apart from the Sunday liturgy?

c) How is our liturgical chanting, and how much is it contributing to worship in spirit and truth?

d) How much training for participation in the liturgical life do we offer to our children?

e) How deeply do we know the essentials of our worship?

f) What are our Churches as buildings, as interiors, as places conducive to an encounter with God?

These are the questions worth pondering and worth following up in our life as communities, Dioceses, and as an Archdiocese. We have to make worship a central issue for every community, an issue for study, planning and work. Let us survey the available means at our disposal, i.e. videocassettes, CDs, etc. related to worship; Let us make a methodical, well organized and consistent effort to bring to the worship of the Church all the people of the community, to increase attendance to its fullness; to take special care for the full participation of the children in the liturgical life; and to think of what you would do if you knew that your community was the last Orthodox community on earth and that the survival and the future of Orthodox worship were totally dependent on your actions.

g) As an Archdiocese we plan to work intensely and methodically on that issue since we have made the liturgical-prayer expression of our Orthodox faith one of our major priorities. The Holy Eparchial Synod of the Greek Orthodox Archdiocese of America with its special committee will proceed with concrete studies and projects in order to facilitate the work of liturgical uniformity, liturgical awareness, liturgical education, liturgical publications, and liturgical enhancement on all levels. This is a formidable task which will need time to fully develop; but we, with the dynamic assistance of our clergy and laity, are determined to work hard in a sustained and passionate effort to make our invaluable worshipping tradition a reality that is alive for today and for the new century, to make it an ageless tradition in the new millennium.

2. The Tradition of Faith as Love

Moving now to the second major task related to the ageless tradition of faith as love, we could propose some more specific efforts and actions.

a) We could start with trying to make love and unity a priority in our community life. That means involving greater and greater numbers of people in the charitable and service-oriented works of the community. Approach the lonely and isolated. Become aware of the difficulties of our neighbors. Support the families confronted with serious problems. Become conscious of the needs of the elderly. Have our Philoptochos chapters go beyond their routine and think of programs to which they could invite the young adults of the community. Philoptochos must become a terrific school and unit for actions of love and care; it must become an attractive enterprise for dynamic and sometimes restless young ladies. Expand the Philoptochos and make it something that could actively involve all members of the community and give to all parishioners the chance for a fruitful cooperation in the field of service.

b) We could then, as a further step ahead, enlarge our horizons and cultivate in our communities the spirit of becoming aware of needs outside of our own community or even immediate geographical area. Think of the larger Orthodox family; be interested in the life and activities of our brothers and sisters in the various areas of the world. At the same time, transform our love and caring feelings into acts of stewardship, and realize that stewardship in the Church is not simply a monetary contribution done sometimes in a mentally detached or distant way, but a real art exhibiting care for the Church on a constant basis, as a continuous offering of goods, time, money, prayers, and any type of assistance.

c) There is, among others, one more issue that needs to become a priority for establishing faith as love. This is the family. The family is a fundamental unit within the Orthodox community, a unit with priceless value. The family is the strongest constitutive element in a parish. The contemporary Greek American Orthodox family must be the primary object of our love and care. I should like to particularly underline the care for the so-called "mixed marriages." It is time to warmly embrace this kind of family which constitutes the large majority of our families. We routinely talk about them as a problem. We must start talking about them as an opportunity for showing the power of love and understanding. We must intensify the efforts of the mixed marriage families to connect all of their members with our Church, to bring their children to the embrace of our *Ecclesia*. Here is a bright opportunity to manifest faith as loving care. Through a significant grant from Leadership 100, the Archdiocese is now in a position to have a program which will deal exclusively and in depth with issues related to mixed marriages. This program is a very promising program which has the potential to enlarge its scope and its radius of activity and to cover more and more issues connected to the mixed marriage families. If we direct a considerable part of our eagerness to assist and to serve the mixed marriage families, we might very well contribute to the transformation of a problem into a real blessing and an opportunity for promoting the Gospel of Christ, a Gospel proclaiming faith as love.

3. The Tradition of Faith as Truth

Coming now to the end of this address, and in dealing with the third task related to the ageless tradition of faith as truth, we may offer the following proposals:

a) On the parish level we should have an ongoing activity offering to the people the opportunity to learn the real contents of our faith as truth. The Church is a school of faith; she is a teaching institution and a training place for the truth. We ordinarily talk about the duty of the Church to offer the Sunday School opportunity to the children. The adults too have the right to be more informed about the truth proclaimed by the Church, to know exactly and fully the fundamental tenets of our Orthodox Faith. This is a vital function that must be active in every parish. Just remember: the parish is the school of the truth of God, and it should act like that, on a continuous and systematic basis. Saint Basil the Great and Saint John Chrysostom gathered the faithful every day and taught them and introduced them to the depths of the divine truth deposited in the Gospel and in the tradition of the Church. They knew extremely well that they could not omit such an important work every day. Our parishes, our Church in America, have to look very carefully at that Patristic model. As an Archdiocese we will try to provide the proper means for such a task.

b) On the level of the National Ministries, we have to think very seriously of a unique institution that plays a pivotal role in guarding, preserving, and promoting faith as truth: Hellenic College and Holy Cross

Greek Orthodox School of Theology. It is at Holy Cross that our priests have been trained in order to be teachers of the divine truth revealed by Christ and given to the Church. It is in that sacred place that the truth of faith is studied, analyzed, transmitted and presented in all its richness, in all its amazing contents, in all its exciting and inspiring history. It is in the very same place that the truth as ageless tradition of our Hellenic heritage is cultivated and abundantly offered both as language and as historical content and culture.

How much is this jewel of our Church in America our real concern? How much actual support does Hellenic College and Holy Cross receive from the Greek American Community? We must confess that the answer to those questions is not encouraging, as the history of this institution shows. We have a new, vigorous, heartfelt, and enthusiastic start. Hellenic College and Holy Cross must become an important priority for the faithful and the communities of our Archdiocese, because it constitutes the basic center of the Church in which faith as truth is the unique and indispensable issue. We have to strengthen it in view of the demanding years to come. We must render it, with the help of our God who is the Truth, the number one center in the world for the study of the truth of faith and the tradition of our universal Hellenic heritage.

As a Greek American Orthodox Community abundantly blessed by God, as a Church destined by the grace of God to be His witness in the Western Hemisphere, we are facing the challenging new millennium with a triple task ahead: The task of offering to our contemporary American society our ageless traditions of faith as worship, faith as love, and faith as truth in an alive, convincing, and rejuvenating way. But faith as worship, love, and truth ultimately is faith in Jesus Christ, Who is the same yesterday, today, and forever: Ἰησοῦς Χριστὸς ἐχθὲς καὶ σήμερον ὁ αὐτὸς καὶ εἰς τοὺς αἰῶνας (Hebrews 13:8), as the Holy Scripture says. He is all our Church traditions epitomized in one ageless tradition, the one and only always dynamic, fresh, liberating, never changing, never fading away, and never dying. It is this Christ that we offer as an eternal, unchanging, and energizing reality to a constantly changing, confused, and aging world.

We are the carriers of His Holy face shining in the darkness; we are His feet which run to the places of the lost and the afflicted and the needy; we are His hands which gave and healed with a gentle touch; we are His mouth which blessed and uttered only the truth. We are His messengers and His ambassadors among our brothers and sisters who come in contact with us.

Saint Paul in one of his letters exhorted the Christians: *Brethren, stand firm and hold to the traditions:* Ἄρα οὖν, ἀδελφοί, στήκετε καὶ κρατεῖτε τὰς παραδόσεις ἃς ἐδιδάχθητε εἴτε διὰ λόγου εἴτε δι᾽ ἐπιστολῆς ἡμῶν (2 Thessalonians 2:15). Yes! Brothers and sisters, stand firm and hold to the ageless traditions. Stand firm and hold to Jesus Christ, the one superb, ageless, and ever-young tradition. A tradition for a creative life in the new millennium and in any millennium from here and now to eternity. And may this Christ, our Lord and God, be with you and your families and your beloved ones today and tomorrow and beyond any limit in time and space.

Offering Our Orthodox Faith to Contemporary America

36th Clergy-Laity Congress Keynote Address

Los Angeles, California
July 1, 2002

Introduction

The Lord said to His disciples, *Peace be with you. As the Father sent me, even so I send you* (John 20:21). This was the great and unique apostolic commission given by the risen Christ to His disciples, a commission that has changed the world.

The Lord says to us today, July 1, 2002, here in Los Angeles, "Peace be with you. As the Father sent me, even so I send you."

This is our great and holy commission. And this is the essential meaning of the phrase "Offering our Orthodox Faith to Contemporary America," the phrase which constitutes the theme of our 36th Biennial Clergy-Laity Congress. "Offering our Orthodox Faith to Contemporary America" means to respond dynamically, creatively and consistently to the holy call that Christ addresses to us: *As the Father sent me, even so I send you.*

God the Father sent to us Christ, the Son. He offered Him to us, to all humanity, to the whole world, so that we may have abundant life, enduring peace and eternal salvation.

But then, Christ our God sends us to the world, to our fellow human beings, specifically, to the people of contemporary America. He sends us to do what He did, to bring the joyful and saving message of the Gospel, to offer the unfailing love of Christ, the fullness of His life and His unwavering truth. We are entrusted by Jesus Christ with the awesome mission and the sacred task to do what He did, to offer wholeheartedly what He offered, without hesitation and without reservations or conditions. We are entrusted by Him to continue His work which He sealed with His sacrificial death on the Cross and His glorious Resurrection. We are called by Him to be at any place and at any time; but particularly, we are called to be here in America, today, His visible, touchable, life-giving presence.

Beloved and respected Hierarchs, priests and deacons, lay brothers and sisters, I greet you this morning warmly; and I embrace you with reverence as this visible and touchable presence of Christ, as ambassadors of God, commissioned by Him and gathered here to this holy and sacred meeting of our Archdiocese, our 36th Biennial Clergy-Laity Congress. Welcome to the city of the Angels as angels, as messengers of Christ the Lord.

Growth and Progress Since the 2000 Congress

Two years have passed since our last meeting in Philadelphia. These two years were filled with activities, events and growth, difficulties and progress, joys and sorrows; years filled with explosive death on September 11, 2001, but also with explosive life. God gave us much more than all that we ask or think (cf. Ephesians 3:20). He gave us the grace to be able to say with St. Paul, *In all things we are more than conquerors through Him* (i.e. Christ) *who loved us* (Romans 8:37).

During the past two years, God offered us a multitude of gifts, a plethora of blessings. It would take long hours even to enumerate them briefly. But allow me to bring back from memory just a few of these blessings as indications of the intense love and graciousness of God, and as items for a warm thanksgiving prayer.

1) Six churches were consecrated, and two had Thyranixia, or opening ceremonies, in various parts of the country: New Orleans, Louisiana; Cardiff-by-the-Sea, California; Elkins Park, Pennsylvania; Annapolis, Maryland; Bayard, Nebraska; Dallas, Texas; Port Jefferson, New York; and Naples, Florida. In almost all of the cases the consecrated churches belong to elaborate building complexes, including community centers, classrooms, gymnasiums and office space. This shows a tremendous level of activity by our communities. In addition to the consecration of churches we had inaugurations of community halls, cultural centers, school classrooms or groundbreaking ceremonies for similar projects in places like Houston, Texas; Staten Island, New York; Waterbury, Connecticut; Little Rock, Arkansas; and Denver, Colorado. At this moment significant activity is taking place all over the USA related to build-

ing new churches, or expanding old ones and constructing buildings and facilities in order to accommodate the ever-increasing needs of the communities. Just in our immediate vicinity here in Los Angeles, in the suburb of Downey, we visited last Friday evening a new, magnificent church under construction. We offer thanks to God for this building and for the expanding activity of our Greek Orthodox Archdiocese.

2) Three new Bishops have been ordained and have been given to the Church. They are the Chief Secretary of our Holy Synod, Bishop Gerasimos of Krateia; the Chancellor of our Holy Archdiocese, Bishop Savas of Troas; and the Director of the Philanthropic work of our Holy Archdiocese, Bishop Andonios of Phasiane. They are gifted and dedicated Hierarchs, who will direct important areas of our Church ministries and serve as Auxiliary Bishops, thus covering vital pastoral and spiritual needs of our communities.

In addition to the bishops, we have had during the same period of the last two years an impressive number of ordinations to the priesthood and to the diaconate. Graduates of our Holy Cross School of Theology of previous years are expressing the willingness to be ordained and serve. At the same time, the percentage of current students ready to commit themselves to the priesthood is rapidly rising. In the two-year period between Philadelphia and Los Angeles we have had 24 ordinations to the diaconate, and 18 ordinations to the priesthood. We give thanks to God for our new bishops, priests and deacons.

3) In the 35th Clergy-Laity Congress in Philadelphia, we reported a sizeable debt from the past which weighed heavily on our Archdiocese, drastically hampering our work and ministries. A quiet effort was made which started with the members of the previous Archdiocesan Council and continued with the members of the present one. The eagerness of the truly distinguished members of our Church to assist with the task of eliminating this debt was amazing. Here, a remarkable phenomenon emerged, and something unexpected happened. Who would really think that people would give large amounts of money for the dissolution of past loans, deficits and debts? However, the unexpected happened! Between Philadelphia of 2000 and Los Angeles of 2002, within less than two years, some astonishingly generous brothers offered more than five million dollars in donations, thus radically reducing our debt—quite a blessing. Just last April, one such truly noble brother came up to me after a meeting and said: "I know that we have still a remaining debt of 1.5 million dollars to a bank. I think our dignity, our identity, as the Greek Orthodox Archdiocese of America obliges us to eliminate it as soon as possible." "For this reason," he added, "please accept a half million dollar donation from me, but anonymously, toward this goal." We give thanks to God for the very noble souls, the true champion contributors of more than five million dollars towards the elimination of the heavy debt which tormented our Archdiocese.

4) September 11, 2001, was a day of death, darkness and unbelievable pain. As a Greek Orthodox Communi-

ty we lost approximately 25 members of our community. The number of persons who were lost might have been more, but unfortunately there is no secure data available. May the memory of our brothers and sisters slaughtered on September 11 be eternal. At the same, exceedingly painful time, however, God granted to our Church the opportunity to offer love, comfort, and assistance in the midst of death, destruction and unbearable pain.

September 11 gave to our Church the sacred occasion to rise up to an admirable level of sensitivity, care and offering in may ways: continuous prayer services, blood donations, supporting and counseling availability, and fundraising for the families of the victims, especially the orphans of the tragedy. I personally witnessed the tremendous outpouring of love demonstrated by our parishes and individually by members of our Church, both clergy and laity. It will take not hours but days and months to speak adequately and to report accurately the many touching stories and incidents in which our Greek Orthodox people showed unusually high human qualities of love, generosity and valiance. Let me temporarily close this subject by also giving you two specific numbers. The one is the amount collected in the September 11 Relief Fund: $2,050,000. The other is the St. Nicholas Fund which has been assisted by unexpected sources: $1,300,000. We give thanks to God for deeming us worthy as the Greek Orthodox Archdiocese of America to offer a strong witness of love and faith in the midst of a catastrophic event of huge proportions such as the September 11 terrorist attack.

5) Another special blessing during this two-year period has been the progress at our Hellenic College and Holy Cross School of Theology. A concerted effort by our bishops, priests, and communities and various individuals, together with the substantial assistance of a generous offering of scholarships by Leadership 100 resulted in a doubling of the number of first year students, especially in the School of Theology for the academic year 2001-2002. We have the same phenomenon for the academic year 2002-2003. This practically means that we reasonably expect a dramatic increase of people who are preparing for the priesthood and, thus, will address a vital need of our Church in America. We give thanks to God for the progress of our sacred institution of Hellenic College and Holy Cross Greek Orthodox School of Theology.

6) Among the special blessings of these past two years, we should also include the activities of our Archdiocese related to SCOBA. IOCC (International Orthodox Christian Charities), which this year completed ten years of existence, continues to develop and increase its activities to a considerable degree, spending millions of dollars in assistance to areas of disaster and urgent needs around the world. The same holds true for the OCMC (Orthodox Christian Mission Center), which at this point in time has fifty-four of our people fully working in the missionary field outside of the USA and supports financially many Orthodox Churches in Africa, the Far East, and Albania. OCMC has an annual budget of approximately two million dollars, which is increasing, a fact

indicative of its activities and bright prospects. We give thanks to God for the work of IOCC and OCMC.

Offering Our Orthodox Faith to Contemporary America

As the Greek Orthodox Church we have been the blessed recipients of the precious and unique gifts of God for the past two thousand years all over the world, and for the past one hundred plus years here in America, starting with our heroic pioneers. Today, in view of such an amazing past loaded with gifts and blessings, in view of the progress and astonishing achievements of our community, and in view of the immediate and the distant future, we hear again and again the commission of our Lord: *Peace be with you. As the Father sent me, even so I send you* (John 20:21). This is the commission to continue with more intensity, creativity and effectiveness, the offering of our Orthodox Faith to contemporary America.

What are the prospects before us? How do we see such an offering on our part? What is the true vision of transforming a divine mandate into powerful action?

1) Offering our Orthodox Faith to contemporary America begins with each one of us individually. The Lord Jesus Christ sends personally every member of our Church to offer the treasures of the Orthodox Faith to the people we meet, to the people who constitute contemporary America. He gives us the privilege to share with others the treasures of the absolute and liberating truth of God and the infinite, life-giving love of Christ.

Are we ready and well prepared as individuals to respond to such an awesome call? Are we growing in the knowledge of Christ and in a sustained, personal, close relationship with Him? Is our knowledge of the truth of God adequately advanced? Are we well aware of our Hellenic Orthodox tradition? Is our individual life of worship and prayer sufficiently rich? Are we in a state of continuous growth in our love and care for others who are assuredly contemporary Americans? If our Orthodox Faith is not organically and inseparably related to our personal life, there is no real way to offer it to anyone. In the final analysis, we cannot offer our faith to contemporary America; we cannot be ambassadors of Christ; we cannot be the true, whole image of Christ if we are not personally and fully committed to Him. Such a commitment must be characteristic of each and every member of our Church if we are serious about offering our Orthodox Faith to contemporary America.

2) The commission, however, to share what we have and to give what we have generously received from God, the commission to offer our Orthodox Faith to contemporary America, goes beyond individuals and addresses the Church as such. The center of the Church as a witness of faith is the parish, the community of believers gathered around the Eucharistic holy table. It is the parish, it is the local community which has been, is, and will forever be the central, indispensable agent for offering our Orthodox Faith to contemporary America.

This 36th Clergy-Laity Congress should be the Congress which will cultivate the awareness of the tremendous importance of the parish, of the need to support the parish with all possible means, to help develop its life and activities, to make the parish a powerful witness and passionate promoter of Orthodox Faith and Tradition. In this Congress we should designate the two years between now and the next Biennial Congress as years of an intense care for the parish in order to facilitate its unrestricted growth.

The Archdiocese as a whole, and the Dioceses as parts of the whole, must focus on the parishes, constantly assist them, consistently serve them, providing them with all means available so that they can be true witnesses of the Gospel, genuine transmitters of the life of Jesus and His salvation offered to all people and to contemporary America.

As the Archdiocese, we will intensify and enlarge our efforts to be focused on our parishes; we will steadily persist in our task to be of substantive and effective assistance to our communities. With the help of God we intend to establish a relationship in which the primary concern of the Archdiocese is to serve the parish, to promote and enhance the life and activities of local communities all over the country. Only strong, healthy and constantly developing church communities can offer our Orthodox Faith to contemporary America in a realistic way. But how are we going to strengthen and develop our parishes? What are the specific steps we intend to take in order to make them units of vitality and powerful witnesses of faith?

3) In order to advance the real serving attitude of the Archdiocese toward our parishes, we have already started, or are about to start, a number of specific major projects. Allow me to report briefly on them.

(a) The existing Department of Family and Marriage at the Archdiocese, dealing mostly with cases of the so-called mixed or interfaith marriages, is rapidly developing and becoming the Center for Family Care. It will be located and will operate at Saint Basil Academy in Garrison, NY. The Center for Family Care will develop programs and resources that will address questions and issues related to preparation for marriage, marital difficulties, interfaith marriages, clergy families, and families of divorce. It will also produce video, audio and printed material relevant to the above mentioned areas, and it will make these resources available to parishes and families. It will organize seminars and educational opportunities that will address areas of family life and development and will make available counseling possibilities via telephone or the Internet. All of these resources will be available and easily deliverable to our parishes so that the families within each community will become the object of constant and methodical attention, care and assistance. Our vision and our objective in this instance is to create, with the help of God, a Center for Family Care that will be a model institution for the advancement of healthy, happy, and dynamic Orthodox families, and for the full incorporation of interfaith marriages into the life of each and every parish. Our vision is to create a model institution, which will be a leader in the field of family care among the Christians denominations of contemporary America.

(b) The Youth Department is also being restructured and expanded so that it will be able to offer to our parishes the necessary help in organizing ministry related to the youth. In cooperation with the Department of Religious Education and the Greek Education Department, which provide hundreds of educational resources, the Youth Department will assist the communities in their tasks related to JOY, GOYA and YAL. Particular attention has been given to YAL, a vital young age group of our Church, which probably has not been provided with the proper means for a healthy growth in recent years. Particular attention is also being given to the revitalization of the Orthodox Campus Fellowship, a ministry under SCOBA, which is directed towards the thousands of Orthodox students in our colleges and universities. Our vision and our objective is to overcome the sad phenomenon observed in almost all religious entities in America, according to which adolescents and young adults in the age bracket of 16 to 30 drop out of their respective religious communities. A mighty way to offer our Orthodox Faith to contemporary America is to demonstrate as a fact that Orthodoxy can create a vigorous and productive youth that remains faithfully within the Church and constitutes her most exciting and effective age group. The steady orientation of the Youth Department will be to the youth of the parish, and it is to the parish that the pertinent activities will be incessantly channeled.

(c) There is a third major development in organizing important Archdiocesan services for the parishes, thus rendering our offering of our Faith to contemporary America more effective. This is the creation of the Philanthropy Department. The charitable work of the Church is a huge area of action. Our Ladies Philoptochos Society has been doing a truly remarkable work over the years, for which we all are very proud. The area of philanthropy, however, presents us with the potential for further, unlimited growth, encompassing vital needs of contemporary America. The case for our aging people for instance, is such an immediate need. Several of our communities have already established various types of homes for the aged. We have, for instance, a central place of this type in Yonkers, NY, St. Michael's Home. But the needs are overwhelming. The Philanthropy Department will aim to support all pertinent efforts, providing the appropriate resources and guidance.

The same Department will further assist all philanthropic tasks undertaken by the communities, developing at the same time a complete file of all philanthropic activities of the parishes. This way pertinent information and experience emanating from local efforts could be communicated nationally to all parishes for possible developments of similar tasks.

There are cries for help coming from various places: people with special needs, people who are hungry and poor, people who are sick and abandoned. They are reaching out, begging for support. The new department will gradually and systematically enlarge its realm of activity and do anything possible to assist our parishes in their sacred efforts to offer our Orthodox Faith to contemporary America in the form of philanthropic witness, in the form of a limitless love in the name of Christ and in continuity with His unique ministry of love, compassion, and care. Our vision and objective here is to project, through our Parishes, Dioceses and Archdiocese, a witness of our Orthodox Faith to contemporary America by means of offering love the way that Christ offered it to the world.

(d) The fourth major project, a project of truly impressive proportions, concerns the demanding task of Communications. Here we have the whole area of web sites and the Internet in general, video and audio productions, the preparation and distribution of printed material, and our relations with the media.

Already, our progress in these truly critical areas is well-advanced, as we are providing significant services to our parishes. We are in the joyful position to announce that the new and upgraded web site of the Archdiocese was released last week. Our goal, however, is to increase this offering and provide our parishes, on a regular basis, with substantive material which will be of immediate use for them. For instance, we plan to issue formatted material to be used for the weekly bulletin of the community; to make available homiletical, educational, and catechetical material and other resources; and to help parishes with information related to pastoral, philanthropic and evangelistic ministry. The communications opportunities, immediately accessible to our communities, will be one of the most dynamic services of the Archdiocese, and certainly it will be a central task in the present and in the years to come.

We strongly believe that with the multifarious assistance provided by the Communications Department to our parishes, they will be in a better position to offer our Orthodox Faith to contemporary America. Our vision and objective in this case is to develop and to use a communications system that will be a powerful vehicle for the transmission of the Gospel message to the hearts of our fellow Americans, for the transmission of the very voice of Christ to the ears and the hearts of the people of the world.

(e) The last major development related to our mission for offering the witness of our Orthodox Faith to today's American society, is the intensification and growth of the educational activities of our Church. There is an urgent need to advance the knowledge of our Orthodox Tradition and our truly universal Hellenic heritage. This is a splendid heritage that is integrally connected with our Orthodox Faith, encompassing vast areas of culture, civilization and language. Our heritage is not narrowly ethnic but belongs to the whole civilized world. There is an urgent need for creating a body of faithful who will be truly illumined, truly educated, truly and fully informed about our Greek Orthodox identity.

Through our unique institution of Hellenic College and Holy Cross School of Theology, through our Departments of Religious Education and Greek Education, through our schools, and through all other means available; we plan to promote education, *paideia,* as a central, vital issue in the life of our Church here. This is an issue that has to be nurtured and cultivated in our parishes, thus enabling them to promote effectively our faith and to offer it to contemporary America, the place of astonishing progress in matters of science and learning.

Conclusion

We have presented five major developments of great importance for offering our Orthodox Faith to contemporary America:

1) The Center for Family Care;

2) The restructuring and intensification of the work of Youth Ministry;

3) The creation of the Philanthropy Department;

4) The reorganizing of the Communications Department for maximum, state of the art performance; and

5) The enhancement and promotion of our educational activities.

The importance of the above-mentioned developments is also seen in that these developments are fully directed toward our parishes and for their benefit.

There is, however, another aspect of importance related to these developments which I am in the exceedingly blessed position to share with you today. There are distinguished members of our Church here in America who are deeply appreciative of such developments and such progress, which shows the potential for the unprecedented growth of our parishes and our Archdiocese. These remarkable brothers, these true pillars of the work of the Church, have declared their willingness and their commitment to support these projects and programs financially. And the commitment is millions of dollars—a truly tremendous contribution that is readily available.

But this is not a matter for a very few major donors. This is a matter for all of our faithful. The projects we are talking about must be warmly embraced by all, strongly supported by all, and passionately promoted by all. They are projects aimed at offering our Orthodox Faith to contemporary America in a well-focused, carefully balanced, and all-encompassing manner.

The results might far exceed our thoughts, expectations and visions. The results might not be many, but one: the creation of a new era in the history of Orthodoxy, the creation of a new model in ecumenical Orthodoxy, the model of Greek American Orthodoxy of the twenty-first century and beyond. Who knows if God has not sent us in this blessed country at this time, at this hour, precisely in order to offer this model of universal Orthodoxy, a model destined to carry the authentic, whole, life-giving and holy voice of Christ to every person in every place, but primarily here in contemporary America.

We are invited in the name of Christ our Lord and God, and with His invincible power, to have the vision to work and to pray for an America which will become the place of a shining, pioneer, model, and leading Orthodox Faith. This invitation might have been issued some time ago. Today, however, in this 36th Clergy-Laity Congress of our Archdiocese, it is heard clearly and loudly. We have to respond to God. We have to work with Him. We have to create with Him a shining Orthodoxy for America.

Building Communities of Faith and Love: Orthodox Parishes in Worship and Ministry

37th Clergy-Laity Congress Keynote Address

New York, New York
July 26, 2004

1. Introduction

I greet you with the opening lines of thankfulness of St. Paul's second epistle *To the Thessalonians*, from which also the biblical theme for our Clergy-Laity Congress has been taken: *We are bound to give thanks to God always for you, because your faith is growing abundantly, and the love of every one of you for one another is increasing. Therefore, we ourselves boast of you in the Churches of God...* (2 Thessalonians 1: 3-4). Thanks for your faith and love; thanks for keeping the Gospel present and alive among us, bearing fruit and continuously growing.

2. Our Congress in Context

Our 37th Clergy-Laity Congress convenes at a time of significant events and unusual conditions, both domestically and internationally. We are aware of them, and our work here could profit by keeping them in mind as challenges. Allow me to mention two, selected from several: a) the Olympic Games in Athens in just three weeks, and b) the Presidential election this coming November. Both have an easily discernible common element: competition, athletic or political.

But, there is something beyond competition as such, and this is the striving for excellence; excellence in athletic achievements as in the case with the Olympics; excellence in serving the people and the country as in the case of the presidential race. The Athens Olympics and the Presidential election offer to us a strong challenge for striving and competing for excellence in what we are doing as Church. Should we not consider, seriously and responsibly, our present Clergy-Laity Congress as a God-given opportunity for setting a record of excellence, for establishing a model of a truly God-inspired meeting?

There is, however, more than being aware of the constant challenges for excellence, like the above-mentioned. There is the awareness of the huge problems that beset our society, our country, and our world today. We are painfully conscious of them: problems of terrorism causing insecurity; problems of wars, conflicts, or threatening conditions in the Middle East, the Far East, Africa, even Europe; problems of the deconstruction of institutions like family or religion; problems of rampant corruption, exploitation of the environment, and increasing violations of human rights; problems of an alarming increase of the level of poverty, famine and fatal diseases, especially in underdeveloped countries.

In our meetings at the present 37th Clergy-Laity Congress, we have to remain alert and conscious of the problem-loaded reality in which we live, as well as the challenge for excellence. And we have to remember that we are called to offer, by what we think, say, plan, and do, the Orthodox Christian response to the problems and to the challenges. And this is a real work.

On that issue, the theme of our Congress provides us with some interesting suggestions for relevant work and action. Let us take a closer look at this theme.

3. A Short Biblical Analysis of the Congress' Theme

The Congress' theme reads, "Building Communities of Faith and Love: Orthodox Parishes in Worship and Ministry." First, note that work and action are being described here with the verb *to build*. "Building Communities, etc." It is important that the action be a very positive, beautiful and creative action. When we build, we bring something into existence for a purpose. The action is an edifying one, an enhancing one, not a catastrophic, demeaning, or negative one. But then, what is the object of building? Let us briefly analyze it by using some examples from the Bible, the New Testament.

a) First: Build communities of F a i t h. What kind of faith? Here is an answer through an example from the Gospel of St. Matthew: *Jesus said to the disciples, "Truly I say to you, if you have faith as a grain of a mustard seed, you will say to this mountain, move from here to there, and it will move; and nothing will be impossible to you"* (Matthew 17:20).

This is the kind of faith that we must build in our communities. It is a faith exhibiting the extraordinary power of God and making our communities places of the revelation and action of God's power in many ways. This is a faith able to move even mountains, powerful enough to overcome even the barrier of the impossible.

b) The second, next object of building: Communities of L o v e. What kind of love? This time, let us hear St. Paul as he speaks to the Corinthians: *If I speak in the tongues of men and of angels, but have not love, I am a noisy gong or a clanging cymbal. And if I have prophetic powers, and understand all mysteries and all knowledge, and if I have all faith, so as to remove mountains, but have not love, I am nothing. If I give away all I have, and if I deliver my body to be burned, but have not love, I gain nothing. Love is patient and kind; love is not jealous or boastful; it is not arrogant or rude. Love does not insist on its own way; it is not irritable or resentful; it does not rejoice at wrong, but rejoices in the right. Love bears all things, believes all things, hopes all things, endures all things. Love never ends* (I Corinthians 13:1-8).

Can we build this type of love in our communities? We should not even ask the question. We have to build this love, if we believe in a God who is love.

c) The third object of building: Orthodox parishes in W o r s h i p. In this instance, we hear the directive of the Lord Himself who declared, *God is spirit and those who worship Him must worship in spirit and truth* (John 4:24).

Our communities are communities in worship of a God who is the absolute Spirit and the perfect Truth.

Therefore, our worship should reflect the highest, strongest, and most refined kind of spirituality, and, at the same time, be permeated by the truth, the whole truth of our being, our life, our community, and our world. This is the true meaning of the phrase, "Building Orthodox Parishes of Worship."

d) The fourth object of building: Orthodox parishes in M i n i s t r y. Here again, we hear the voice of the Lord. It is the commissioning of the disciples by Christ Himself before His Ascension: *All authority in heaven and on earth has been given to me. Go therefore and make disciples of all nations, baptizing them in the name of the Father and of the Son and of the Holy Spirit, teaching them to observe all that I have commanded you, and lo, I am with you always, to the close of the age* (Matthew 28:18-20).

The ministry solemnly described here is a ministry of offering both the witness of the Gospel everywhere, and the teaching of the genuine and full way of the Christian life. Both aspects, namely, proclaiming and teaching, involve complex issues, processes, and various forms of ministry; but they are absolutely indispensable to a creative and effective ministry which is in continuity with the ministry of Christ Himself and His Apostles.

It is in the biblical spirit of faith and love, worship and ministry, described above, that we meet in this 37th Clergy-Laity Congress.

4. Encouraging Events Between 2002 and 2004

We meet in order to be together and to discuss

and plan the dynamic, holy and noble action for building, with the help of God, Communities of Faith and Love, Orthodox Parishes in Worship and Ministry. In our God-inspired effort, an effort which continues and intensifies the work done for many years by the faithful people of our Church in America, we are encouraged by some significantly positive events of the past two years. In the period between our last Clergy-Laity Congress in Los Angeles in 2002, and the present one, we noticed with thankfulness to God, among many other things, the following events, indicative of God's grace and love for us, as well as of the truly dedicated and often sacrificial work of our people and of our communities:

a) We noticed the continuous activities of several of our parishes throughout our country in building new churches, new community halls, new school facilities, new summer camps, or in the renovation of existing ones. This constitutes an encouraging activity by our parishes, a veritable blessing.

b) We noticed the increasing auspicious responses to our call for more priests in order to adequately cover the pastoral and spiritual needs of our communities. This was apparent in the comparatively high number of new students in our Holy Cross School of Theology, for now four consecutive years. It is also apparent in the expanding number of ordinations to the priesthood. In the Los Angeles Clergy-Laity, I reported to you that between the years 2000 and 2002, we had 18 ordinations to the priesthood. Today, I am in the blessed position to report to you that in the last two years, i.e., between 2002 and

2004, we have had 24 ordinations to the priesthood, with another 5 pending for approval for ordination. These are truly auspicious and encouraging signs.

c) We noticed during the same two year period an increase of the work in the areas of care for the family, care for the youth, care for planning and developing community assisted outreach and evangelism, and care for providing our communities with more assistance through our website. Here, we deal with issues of vital importance for the Church. I don't want to tire you with statistics, but I have to say that the initiatives taken in the above mentioned areas are noticeable indeed. We already have encouraging results related to those areas.

d) We take note of the fact that in a few months after the Los Angeles Clergy-Laity Congress, the creative and open process related to a revised or new Charter of the Archdiocese, reached its conclusion. Since January of 2003, for one and a half years now, we have as operative and fully functioning, the new Charter granted to us by the Ecumenical Patriarchate. Our Holy Archdiocese of America has been elevated to an Archdiocese consisting of Metropolises and Metropolitans, who constitute the Holy Eparchial Synod. This is a phenomenon unique in the Orthodox Church, since it is only Autocephalous or Autonomous Churches that have Metropolises and Synods comprised of Metropolitans. This is indicative of the love of the Ecumenical Patriarchate for our Church. We have a Charter establishing a definitely enhanced role for our dedicated laity, both in matters of administration of and care for the Archdiocese, and in matters specifically connected with the procedures for the elections of the Metropolitans and the Archbishop. The granting of the Charter gave us the opportunity to proceed, without delay, to the reviewing of the existing Regulations of the Archdiocese, in order to harmonize them with the Charter. After a hard, intensive, and highly commendable work of more than a year by the Archdiocesan Council, a clearly representative body of approximately eighty clergy and lay people, a proposed draft is ready now for discussion and appropriate decisions by the present Congress.

I hope, and if I may, I strongly recommend that, after almost five years of intense, diligent, and responsible work related to the Charter and the Regulations, work that consumed enormous amounts of time and energy, we have come to the point of the inescapable need of concluding the process. There are absolutely vital and crucial tasks related to our God-given existence, function, and mission as the Greek Orthodox Church in America. These tasks urgently demand our attention, our time, and, quite frankly, our exclusive focus. After all, the ultimate, absolute and unchanging Charter and Regulations for us, is the Gospel of Jesus Christ our God and Lord. All the rest is commentary. It is about time now to engage fully in the real work demanded by the Gospel.

e) Among the blessings which occurred in the last two years, and more specifically in the last four months, is the very important changing of the composition of the Holy and Sacred Synod of the Ecumenical Patriarchate.

By an historic and indeed bold decision, the Synod is no longer comprised of twelve Hierarchs residing exclusively in Turkey. Since last March, the Synod has as its members only six Hierarchs residing in Turkey, while another six Hierarchs come from all over the world, i.e. Europe, America, Australia, Asia, etc. The percentage, 50%, is remarkably high, and indicative, of course, of a radical change. I have the great honor to be a member of the Holy and Sacred Synod of the Ecumenical Patriarchate, created under the new participatory formula. I have been already in a number of Synodal meetings in Constantinople, and I have to confess that this participation in the very administration of the Ecumenical Patriarchate constitutes an unprecedented honor and an awesome responsibility for our Archdiocese. Please remember that we are going to be there when any matters whatsoever pertaining to our Church in the United States, are going to be discussed.

f) Let me close the list of significantly positive events and blessings with one more item. This item is the magnificent task of creating a substantive endowment for assistance to our ministries and to our work in general. Under the title, "FAITH: An Endowment for Orthodoxy and Hellenism," ten gentlemen, prominent members of our Church and true champions of faith, decided to offer, each one of them, one million dollars and up, for the establishment of a strong fund for the Archdiocese. The pertinent commitment has reached so far the amount of approximately twenty-five million dollars. The objective is to reach, through a quiet effort of the founding members of the Faith Endowment, the amount of fifty million dollars in a first phase, and one hundred million dollars as an ultimate goal of the founders. The "Faith Endowment", a first in our Archdiocese in terms of magnitude, is a blessing and, at the same time, an open invitation to all the members of our parishes for a more substantive participation in the stewardship of our Church.

5. Focusing on Three Vital Points

"Building Communities of Faith and Love: Orthodox Parishes in Worship and Ministry," is not an easy task. In view of the conditions prevailing in today's society, it becomes a formidable task indeed. But also in view of the continuous rich blessings just described that we have been receiving from God, it becomes a task with open, accessible and very promising goals and perspectives. Allow me, in the last part of my presentation, to focus briefly on three vital points related to the truly holy and exciting task of "Building Communities of Faith and Love, Orthodox Parishes in Worship and Ministry."

a) The kind of communities which we are talking about and dreaming about, cannot be built without strong, sustained, and in-depth education. Our parishes must be parishes of a multi-level, many-sided, educational activity. There must be in every parish a forum, a school, a seminar of continuous adult Orthodox education. The depths and the treasures of our Orthodox Faith and traditions are waiting to be received, explored, and enjoyed by the adult members of our communities, which then will function as open schools for the teaching of genuine and full Orthodoxy. The parish could be, and should be, a standard resource center of Orthodoxy for its members.

Such an effort should also include the educational component of Hellenism, which is part of our tradition. Let me clarify here that the Hellenism we are talking about and which constitutes part of the title of the new Faith Endowment (an "Endowment for Orthodoxy and Hellenism"), is not a nationalistic, chauvinistic entity. It is a designation of a superb synthesis of the Hellenic language, history, and culture that is transnational, undoubtedly universal, and purely diachronic and timeless. It is a synthesis constituting a vital, inseparable component of western civilization, by offering the principles of freedom and democracy, advancement of knowledge and science, and cultivation of what is beautiful in all forms of art. The Hellenic component, as part and parcel of our educational efforts, is therefore an indispensable component in any education worthy of its full name; it is an indispensable component in building for a lasting future, not the passing, present time.

We speak about the need for an adult Orthodox education because we see a deficiency on this issue. The other side of this issue is, of course, children's education. It is unthinkable that there might be communities without an adequate Sunday School and proper Afternoon School. Certainly, it is not realistic, at this stage, to think of a full Day School for all of our more than 500 parishes. But Sunday School and Afternoon School, offering religious education and the cultural education of our heritage, must be a permanent reality of each and every community of our Church.

I would also strongly recommend that we pay much more attention to our young people, to the adolescent members of our parishes. They need an advanced Orthodox education beyond the Sunday or the Afternoon School.

We have to understand, once and for all, that it is simply impossible to "Build Communities of Faith and Love, Parishes of Worship and Ministry," without a strong, continuous educational activity for adults, for young people, and for children in every parish. As the Holy Archdiocese of America, we will intensify and enhance our efforts to facilitate the relevant work of our communities by providing, more and more, the appropriate tools and resources.

b) No matter how strong and well-functioning the infrastructure of a community may be, it cannot be a community of Faith and Love, Worship and Ministry, without strong and healthy families as its constitutive parts. The building blocks of a parish are its families. What the cells are for a living organism, the families are for a living community. The care for the family is a priority in building true Church communities. Here, we talk about care for the endangered family, for the dysfunctional family, for the healthy family, for the family at the brink of divorce, for a single parent family, for the priestly family, for the beginning family. Of paramount importance is the care for the so-called intermarried family, since in this case we face not only the basic needs of an ordinary family, but increased needs, especially catechetical needs and additional relational challenges. The care for the family is a priority imposed not only by our faith, but also by the terrible crisis surrounding the family. Listen to some randomly selected recent statistics:

Number of unwed births of children:
    In 1960 = 224,300   In 2000 = 1,374,043
Cohabitation:
    In 1960 = 439,000   In 2000 = 4,736,000
Divorce:
    50% of marriages starting today are projected to end in divorce.
Children in single parent families:
    In 1960 = 5,829,000   In 2000 = 19,220,000

This set of data explains why, in a Gallup Poll of January 3, 2003, the Family was ranked number one in importance among the most important aspects of life with a response of 97%, followed by a 90% for health, 73% for work, 67% for money, 65% for religion, and 59% for leisure. The emphasis on the importance of the family is astonishing.

We are going to dedicate the next year to the family, with an elaborate number of specific measures and happenings. But the care for the family should constitute a permanent activity for the Parish, and toward that end we will try to assist our communities by offering all possible means. The goal is to make the families Churches at home, κατ' οἶκον ἐκκλησίας (Romans 16:5). The Center for the Care for the Family has been diligently and methodically working, in spite of the lack of the necessary funding, for its full development. We already had, last Saturday, an opportunity to see part of the work of the Center for the Care for the Family in an extensive, all-day educational program. We will see and hear more during the present Clergy-Laity Congress. The important thing is to be aware of the priority of the family in the effort of building Communities of Faith and Love.

c) I close this address with a third, vital point. A Community of Faith and Love, a Parish in Worship and Ministry, cannot be built without having a steady experience of outreach, of evangelism directed lovingly towards those outside the Church. The theme of this year should be interpreted in the spirit of the theme of our Clergy-Laity Congress in Los Angeles: "Offering our Orthodox Faith to Contemporary America." This offering is a fundamental function of the parish. It is the parish that has the possibility to reach out to the non-connected with the Church. There are thousands of people, nominally Greek Orthodox, who have been disconnected, who have been lost in the turmoil of modern life, who might have been disappointed. It is totally unthinkable and unacceptable to have parishes with only one thousand members when they are surrounded by thousands of unchurched Orthodox people. Our communities must look for them, extend a helping hand, bring them to the life-giving embrace of the Church of Christ. This is the way we build communities of ministry.

When St. Paul the great Apostle of Christ was with St. Luke the Evangelist in Troas of Asia Minor, he had a dramatic vision. The relative narrative in the Book of the Acts of the Apostles is a moving and far-reaching text. I read this text now: *And a vision appeared to Paul in the night: a man of Macedonia was standing, beseeching him and saying, "Come over to Macedonia and help us." And when he had seen the vision, immediately we sought to go into Macedonia, concluding that God had called us to preach the Gospel to them* (Acts 16:9-10).

Paul went to Macedonia, to Greece. This started the conversion of Europe to Christianity. We do not need to have a vision like St. Paul. There are plenty; there are in essence millions of people symbolizing the Macedonian of the Pauline vision. And they repeat the same plea: *"Come over to our place and help us."*

I am sure that we hear the pleading voice, and we see the extended hands. It is God's voice Who is calling us to help them, to share the Gospel of Love and Truth with them, to build, with Christ, Communities of Faith and Love, Orthodox Parishes of Worship and Ministry! What a stimulating vision; what a fascinating, creative action! And what a noble mission of excellence and an opportunity for a great achievement for our 37th Clergy-Laity Congress!

May the Lord bless us and keep us. May the Lord make His face to shine upon us and be gracious to us. May the Lord lift up His countenance upon us and give us peace. Εὐλογή-

σαι σε Κύριος καὶ φυλάξαι σε, ἐπιφάναι Κύριος τὸ πρόσωπον αὐτοῦ ἐπὶ σὲ καὶ ἐλεῆσαι σε, ἐπάραι Κύριος τὸ πρόσωπον αὐτοῦ ἐπὶ σὲ καὶ δῴη σοι εἰρήνην (Numbers 6:24-26).

Sharing the Truth of the Gospel and the Love of Christ

38th Clergy-Laity Congress Keynote Address

Nashville, Tennessee
July 17, 2006

1. Introduction

By the grace and love of God, we are together once again for the 38th Clergy-Laity Congress of our Holy Greek Orthodox Archdiocese of America. We are meeting here, in the beautiful and hospitable city of Nashville, Tennessee, in order to translate into projects and actions the theme of our Congress: "Sharing the Truth of the Gospel and the Love of Christ." To do this means sharing the truth and the love of Christ with our brothers and sisters of the Orthodox faith, and with our non-Orthodox, even non-Christian neighbors, colleagues, and citizens of this country, and to people beyond America.

The task is truly monumental. It constitutes a responsible answer to the call for mission addressed to us by the Lord Jesus Christ Himself when He said, "*Go into all the world and preach the Gospel to the whole creation*" (Mark 16:15). Offer the Gospel of the truth, the Gospel of the love of Christ to the ends of the Earth. Share with every human being the supreme joy of the liberating truth and the indescribable experience of the limitless love of Christ.

Viewed from such an awesome perspective, the theme of the present 38th Congress of our Church "Sharing the truth of the Gospel and the love of Christ" becomes a very serious challenge that is best posed as a question: Are we going to deal in our meetings responsibly, bravely, and dynamically with this theme, or are we going to treat it as a nice religious slogan, of a rather decorative nature and of no important consequences for our lives?

I would like for you to keep this question present and active throughout the days of our blessed meetings here. Please let the theme of our Congress be the real focus and the stimulating challenge during our discussions and actions here. Nashville has a big name as a major U.S. center for producing music. Can we not make Nashville also a great place for producing our own Gospel music of truth and love through our 38th Congress?

2. Some events and facts since our last Clergy-Laity Congress in New York 2004

As we start our work here, we remember a number of events and facts which happened in the two years since our last Clergy-Laity Congress.

1) We remember the falling asleep in the Lord of our beloved Archbishop Iakovos of North and South America. A great Church leader of this Archdiocese for thirty-seven years, he left us on April 10 of last year.

Filled with the peace of God, anticipating with joy and faith his encounter with Christ, displaying an amazing dignity up to the last minute of his earthly life, he departed this world praying for us and blessing the name of the Lord. May the memory of Archbishop Iakovos be eternal!

We also remember the falling asleep in the Lord of the beloved Brother Metropolitan Anthony of San Francisco. After a heroic fight against an unexpected deadly form of cancer, he breathed his last on Christmas day in the year 2004 leaving behind the legacy of a dynamic, creative and faithful hierarchical ministry. May his memory be eternal!

We also gratefully remember the priests, presbyteres, archons, and lay leaders of our Archdiocese who offered their noble services to the Church for many years and passed away during the last two years. May their memory also be eternal!

2) We painfully experienced all the above mentioned departures. But the merciful God gave us, at the same time, the comfort and the joy of having a new Metropolitan of San Francisco in the person of Metropolitan Gerasimos, enthroned on April 2 of last year, as well as the gratification of having a good number of new clergy, approximately 40, by ordination or incardination, during the same two-year period. We thank the Lord for these gifts.

3) Following the last Clergy-Laity Congress, we were in the advantageous position of having the revised Regulations approved by our Ecumenical Patriarchate,

which were published and made effective in 2005. Thus, in one booklet of Regulations containing thirty-five articles, we have an excellent tool to help us in our administrative work in the Parishes, the Metropolises, and the Archdiocese in general.

During the same period and in accordance with our Charter (Articles 21 and 15), our Holy Eparchial Synod prepared a) the "General Regulations for the establishment and operation of Holy Monasteries in the Greek Orthodox Archdiocese of America," and b) the "Regulations regarding the Auxiliary Bishops of the Archdiocese." These two new sets of Regulations were approved by the Ecumenical Patriarchate, published and made effective last year. To our Ecumenical Patriarchate, to our Hierarchs, to the members of the pertinent Archdiocesan Committees, to the members of the 35th, 36th, 37th Clergy-Laity Congresses in Philadelphia, Los Angeles, and New York, respectively, and to all Brothers and Sisters who worked so diligently, so responsibly, and so tirelessly for the preparations of the Charter and the various Regulations mentioned above, we express on behalf of our Eparchial Synod our deep gratitude.

4) Since the last Clergy-Laity Congress in New York, our work for our Ecumenical Patriarchate took a different turn. We drastically increased our efforts to have the U.S. Government, the State Department in particular, involved in the hard task of resolving the major issues that infringe upon the religious freedom of our beloved and venerable Ecumenical Patriarchate. At the same time, through the intense and persisting actions

of our Archons of the Ecumenical Patriarchate and with the assistance of other influential people, we expanded our activities in the territory of the European Union aiming at pressing Turkey for the elimination of issues that plague our Ecumenical Patriarchate.

5) During the past two years, in spite of some difficulties, the work that we do, with the help of God, in SCOBA has been steadily progressing. Thus, IOCC (International Orthodox Christian Charities) offered increasing and considerable help in catastrophic cases like Hurricane Katrina and in areas of conflict or war, as seen in Iraq, Israel and the Middle East in general. In 2005 alone, IOCC offered $32 million in services.

On the other hand, OCMC (Orthodox Christian Mission Center) is one more growing activity of SCOBA. At OCMC, beyond their growing important work, they are now in the process of starting to build a new home and center in St. Augustine, Florida, in order to create a training center for people involved in the mission work of our Church in various countries outside the USA.

OCF (Orthodox Christian Fellowship) constitutes another important SCOBA activity. This is an effort to create Orthodox Christian student groups in American colleges and universities. We now have such OCF chapters at 200 universities.

These are a few recent examples of the important work produced by SCOBA through several other activities. This work is a specimen of pan-Orthodox unity and nature. I am mentioning it because by the grace of God our Archdiocese has been playing for years now a central role in it, a role of offering extensive and decisive resources, coordination and personnel. We are responsibly and methodically cultivating the spirit of unity in action among all Orthodox in America in terms of real cooperation and common tasks for the witnessing of Orthodoxy.

6) In the past two years we have seen a significant increase in the philanthropic work of our Church, especially by our Ladies Philoptochos Society. It is noteworthy that in the specific case of unexpected catastrophes, like Hurricane Katrina, our Church as a whole did outstanding work, particularly our National Philoptochos and our Philoptochos chapters of the Metropolis of Atlanta in the district of which the areas of destruction belong. We thank all these noble workers of love and care, and we are grateful to God for them.

7) The year 2005 has been designated as the Year of the Family. Many of the faithful have been working with zeal and patience in programs and activities for family guidance and support. Gratitude belongs to them. But the special care for the family did not end with the closing of the year 2005. It continues undiminished, since the family remains at the center of our attention, love, and care.

I do not want to continue mentioning events and facts of the past two years which are related to important areas of Church life and activities, such as Communications, Religious Education, Greek Education, Finances, Youth, Leadership 100, Faith Endowment, etc. We will have the opportunity to discuss these activities at length in the various meetings at this Congress.

Therefore, let us now proceed to a brief presentation of suggestions for planning and action related to the theme of our Congress, "Sharing the Truth of the Gospel and the Love of Christ."

3. Suggestions related to the theme of this Congress

1) We have plenty of data that helps us by offering pertinent suggestions. We have, in addition, the results of a recent and excellent tool that promises to facilitate our effort; and this is the SWOT survey which was conducted by our Archdiocese in the past months. The SWOT, an acronym for Strengths, Weaknesses, Opportunities and Threats, is a survey that is largely used as an instrument for improvement by various organizations. You will receive a report about the findings and results of our survey, and there will be in our meetings more detailed information on SWOT. At this point allow me to refer only to some basic information from the SWOT survey connected to perceived Strengths, Weaknesses, Opportunities and Threats related to our Archdiocese. This will help us better understand the meaning and the implications of our theme "Sharing the Truth of the Gospel and the Love of Christ."

a) *Perceived as Strengths of the Archdiocese*
- The spiritual leadership of the Archdiocese
- The Orthodox Theology and worship

- The skilled and competent Clergy
- The strong spiritual identity
- The important and unique message
- The electronic media
- The competent volunteers and laity

b) *Perceived as Weaknesses of the Archdiocese*
- Lack of understanding of the Orthodox Faith by the faithful
- Little understanding of Orthodoxy by those outside the Church
- Low awareness of Orthodoxy in America
- Lack of uniform liturgical texts in English
- Inadequate funding
- Poor fiscal planning
- Lack of strategic planning

c) *Perceived as Opportunities for the Archdiocese*
- Marriage between Orthodox and Non-Orthodox
- Emerging technologies and resources
- Increased interest from non-Orthodox
- Ease and utilization of communication media
- Orthodox in key business, political and educational positions
- Increased interest in maintaining fiscal responsibility
- Increasing interest in traditional values and issues of Faith in America

d) *Perceived as Threats to the Archdiocese*
- Number of Orthodox who are not well informed about their Faith
- Archdiocesan financial debt
- Diminishing pool of Clergy
- Increasing secularization
- Legal liabilities
- Weakening of the Institution of Marriage
- Weakening of family structure

2) Keeping in mind the information just presented, we can now present some comments on our theme, "Sharing the Truth of the Gospel and the Love of Christ."

The first question: Do we know the truth of the Gospel, so that we can share it? Do we know the truth of the Orthodox Faith based uniquely on the absolute Truth revealed to the world by the Son of God Jesus Christ in His unchanging, definitive, eternal and universal Gospel? Please, remember what our people said in the SWOT survey about perceived major weaknesses, including the lack of understanding of the Orthodox Faith by our faithful and by the people outside of the Church.

How can we effectively share the truth of the Gospel if we display such fundamental ignorance of it? Ignorance of the truth of the Gospel means, in essence, that we do not know Christ, that we do not know Him. He declared: *I am the Truth* (John 14:6). If He is the Truth of the Gospel and if we do not know it, then we do not know Christ. Practically and urgently, therefore, "Sharing the Truth of the Gospel" means first increasing and improving among our people our knowledge of Christ and of His revealed Truth. As we have emphasized in our last Congress, our parishes should be centers for continuous catechism, education and training for acquiring the needed deep and intimate knowledge of the Lord Jesus Christ and of the truth of His Gospel. Teaching the truth of the Gospel has been an absolute priority in the sacred ministry of Christ Himself, in the apostolic activities, in the attitude of the Fathers, and in the life of the Church throughout a history of almost two thousand years. It must be an absolute priority for us, too.

The question is: Where do we stand on this issue? One could answer that we have our Sunday or Catechetical Schools. Is the work of those Schools satisfactory? We often hear complaints about inadequacy, deficiency, watered down teaching, etc. We need changes here if we intend to teach our children properly the truth of the Gospel. We also have the adults. As The Eparchial Synod, we know that there are parishes in our Church that do praiseworthy work for adult Orthodox education; but such a training and function should be an integral, methodical, and indispensable work in the life of each and every parish. No parish should be left without adult catechism, without offering to grown-ups a constant instruction on the truth of the Gospel.

However, this is only part of the work needed. "Sharing the Truth of the Gospel" also means transmitting it to the people, the communities and the society in general outside our own circle. Are we doing that?

A huge field for such an activity is the intermarried family, which is listed as the top opportunity for our Church in the SWOT survey. It is the top opportunity indeed, because this is a field open and ready for immediate action for sharing the truth of the Gospel, for sharing the joy of Orthodoxy. Such action should be a serious part of the agenda in every parish.

Imagine the excitement of having in each and every parish a full, well organized program for offering to the interfaith family the truth of the Gospel.

Imagine the joy of having in each and every parish, catechetical and Hellenic culture schools to teach effectively the truth of Orthodoxy and the treasures of the universal Greek language and culture!

Imagine the exhilaration of having in each and every parish a school of the Gospel, teaching the adults, in methodically organized courses, the truth of the Gospel as a content of faith. Imagine a continuous adult Gospel education!

Imagine? Why imagine? This is not a matter of imagination. This is a blueprint for action in this next and all future years! This is the expected reality if we intend to fulfill our mission as the Greek Orthodox Church in America.

We know well that in this case we need the proper tools in terms of adequate guidance, pertinent material both in printed and in electronic form, and constant support, including, of course, funds which are also necessary.

3) Our theme, however, speaks also about the love of Christ. "Sharing the love of Christ!" Of course we do that. Every time that we offer assistance to the needy, support to the failing, food and drink to the hungry and thirsty, and compassion to the injured and mistreated, we are automatically sharing the love of Christ, because we do what the Lord Himself would have done under the same circumstances. But "sharing the love of Christ" means more. It means increasing both in terms of quantity and quality our personal sharing of the love of Christ with others; with all others, whether inside or outside of our Church. It also means doing this not only as individuals, but even more as Greek Orthodox communities, as an Orthodox presence in America.

We have been blessed to have in our parishes the dedicated groups of the Ladies' Philoptochos Society. They have offered for seventy-five years significant assistance in matters of philanthropic activity. We wholeheartedly thank them. Sharing, however, the love of Christ with other human beings is not to be limited only to our gracious and dedicated ladies. This is a fundamental commandment of our Lord, a strong sign that we are His disciples and that we belong to His kingdom.

Sharing the love of Christ is the trademark of Orthodoxy. A huge field of action is open in front of us, and we cannot close our eyes and ignore it:

Imagine the number of homes for aged people which we as a Church could build all over America!

Imagine the centers for the daily care for pre-school children that we could open attached to our parishes, thus relieving thousands of working mothers, and connecting thousands of parents to the Church!

Imagine the visiting services that we could offer to many people who live alone and who are sick, and desperately need someone to be with them for one or two hours, to read for them from a good book and to talk to them!

Imagine the opportunities which we could create in our neighborhoods and in our towns by becoming the strong volunteers in initiatives for the relief from catastrophic events of all sorts!

Imagine! Why imagine? This is not a matter of imagination. This is a blueprint showing the potential for action in the forthcoming years.

Of course, in sharing the love of Christ we have a long way to go. But we should not be afraid of the distance. We are challenged to move on, having Christ with us day and night.

4. Epilogue

Thanks be to God Who helps us in "Sharing the Truth of the Gospel and the Love of Christ," in a certain way and to a certain degree. My short and rather telegraphic analysis, however, implies that we need improvement and changes, changes on the personal level and changes on the community level. The efforts for a full and appropriate training and education in matters of our Orthodox Faith, the acquisition and sharing of the truth of the Gospel with others, and the sharing with them of the love of Christ; these efforts need extensive and effective work and resources. They also need generous funding. We know that the resources and the funds for the vital services and ministries of our Archdiocese can and must be found. We are deeply thankful for the constantly displayed generosity of our people as individuals and as communities. But funding should cover the urgent needs of our ministries. And we pray that the present 38th Clergy-Laity Congress will, with the help of the merciful God, proceed with the decisions which are appropriate for the translation of the theme "Sharing the Truth of the Gospel and the Love of Christ," into a living, beautiful reality for our Church and for the glory of God.

In the Gospel of Luke, during the course of a teaching addressed to His disciples, the Lord Jesus Christ raised a totally unexpected and truly terrifying question: *When the Son of Man comes, will He find the faith on earth? Πλὴν ὁ υἱὸς τοῦ ἀνθρώπου ἐλθὼν ἆρα εὑρήσει τὴν πίστιν ἐπὶ τῆς γῆς;* (Luke 18:8). This utterly dramatic question points to the unthinkable possibility that when He appears in His second coming, the Lord might not find the faith on earth: a total disappearance of the faith from the face of the Earth!

The question of the Lord aims not at sending a terrifying signal to us as His disciples. It rather constitutes a strong call for action. Let us then have the boldness to say to Christ, that as far as it depends on us, we will do anything possible and impossible to keep the faith alive to the end of time, to the end of history. With His help, we will be sharing the truth of the Gospel and the love of Christ with every human being, with our children, and with our children's children under all circumstances, under all conditions of the present and the future!

Gather My People to My Home

39th Clergy-Laity Congress Keynote Address

*Washington, D.C.
July 14, 2008*

1. Introduction

Glory, praise and thanksgiving belong to Jesus Christ our loving Lord for gathering us in the illustrious city of Washington, DC, the capital of our Nation, for our 39th Clergy-Laity Congress. What a joy and excitement to meet in the place that produces the most important political and governmental decisions that seriously affect not only America but the entire world! And what a joy and excitement to know that in this great global center, through our Clergy-Laity Congress, we will be able, by the grace of God, to offer our strong witness for our Orthodox Faith: a faith that seems to be needed urgently in our fallen and disoriented world, a faith that gives life to the world because it connects the people to the Son of God, Jesus Christ; and as St. John the Evangelist said in his First Letter, *he who has the Son of God has life, he who has not the Son has not life* (1 John 5:12).

So, here we are in Washington, DC, to offer our witness of a faith that gives life to the people and to the world, and to make the theme of our Congress "Gather

My People To My Home," a theme connecting the people to God, the ultimate source of true life.

2. From Nashville, Tennessee to Washington, DC

Before dealing with the theme of the Congress, I would like to review very briefly with you some of the developments that have occurred between our last 38th Clergy-Laity Congress in Nashville, Tennessee in 2006, and the present one. I am sure there will be pertinent information and discussions in the various committees during our meetings here.

1) The first such development is the increase of the number of the clergy in our Archdiocese. During the past two years 49 new clergy were ordained. To this number we should add another 7 clergy who were incardinated to our Church from other Orthodox jurisdictions, making the total number of new clergy 56. This number 56 for the two year period of 2006-2008, shows a significant progress when compared with 40 ordinations and incardinations that occurred in the two year period of 2004-2006.

During the same period we had the retirement of 21 clergy. Eight of them, however, continue to serve in a certain capacity.

In the course of the same last two years, i.e., from June 20, 2006 to July 6, 2008, we experienced with deep pain the separation by death of 33 beloved and distinguished Priests of our Archdiocese, most of whom were among our retired clergy. Let me read their names as an offering of honor and memory. Their names and the dates of their falling asleep in Christ are as follows:

Siagris, Rev. Fr. Achilles / June 20, 2006
Xenofanes, Rev. Fr. George A. / July 30, 2006
Neofotistos, Rev. Fr. George / August 22, 2006
Chakalos, Rev. Fr. James / September 4, 2006
Mylonas, Rev. Fr. Efstathios / September 22, 2006
Sitaras, Rev. Fr. Nicholas M. / November 26, 2006
Kyriakos, Rev. Fr. Peter N. / December 3, 2006
Thanos, Rev. Fr. George N. / December 16, 2006
Harmand, Rev. Fr. Michael C. / January 18, 2007
Kavadas, Rev. Fr. Demetrios / February 25, 2007
Kapsalis, Rev. Fr. Vasilios / February 26, 2007
Papageorge V. Rev. Fr. Emmanuel / April 12, 2007
Mihalakis, V. Rev. Fr. James / April 22, 2007
Kotzakis, V. Rev. Fr. Lukas / June 8, 2007
Paul, Rev. Fr. John / July 2, 2007
Andrews, Rev. Fr. Dean Timothy / July 18, 2007
Katsoulis, Rev. Fr. Nicholas / August 2, 2007
Koskores, Rev. Fr. Peter B. / September 15, 2007
Maniudakis, Rev. Fr. Chrysostom / October 14, 2007
Gratsias, Rev. Fr. Emmanuel J. / October 16, 2007
Sirigos, Rev. Fr. Anthony C. / November 29, 2007
Kehayes, Rev. Fr. William S. / December 17, 2007
Bartz, Rev. Fr. George / January 15, 2008
Nicozisin, Rev. Fr. George / March 1, 2008
Kalpaxis, Rev. Fr. George / March 8, 2008
Kontogianes, Rev. Dn. John / March 15, 2008
Mamangakis, Rev. Fr. George / March 16, 2008

Michalopulos, Rev. Fr. Michael / April 6, 2008
Kastaris, Rev. Fr. Panagiotis / April 7, 2008
Kogias, V. Rev. Fr. Nectarios / May 7, 2008
Retselas, Rev. Fr. Nicholas / May 22, 2008
Koutoukas, V. Rev. Archimandrite Paul / May 26, 2008
Longos, Rev. Fr. George/ July 6, 2008
May their memory be eternal.

At the same time we have had the special joy of adding a new Bishop to our Church, in the person of Fr. Dimitrios Kantzavelos, the Chancellor of the Metropolis of Chicago, who on December 9, 2006 was ordained Bishop and given the title Bishop of Mokissos.

2) The second development worth mentioning is the significant progress on the financial front: The dramatic reduction of the debt and the payables of the Archdiocese, the closing of the years 2006 and 2007 with almost no deficit, the continuous steady increase of the offerings of our Parishes for the past eight years, the remarkable growth of the funds and the membership of the Archbishop Iakovos Leadership 100 Endowment Fund, and of the Faith Endowment for Orthodoxy and Hellenism and the impressive increase of unrestricted donations. These are some of the data convincingly demonstrating the economic progress particularly achieved in the past two years, a progress that is related also to the success of our newly implemented system for the National Ministries Commitment of our Parishes.

3) The third noticeable development is the progress that has been made in the field of education. This

progress is evident in the writing of new books for kindergarten, and for effectively teaching Greek as a second language for our Greek American children, in the special seminars for teachers organized in our Metropolises, in Greece, and in Cyprus. Progress in education is also seen in the coordinated efforts with the Ministry of Education of Greece relating to computer assisted programs and special educational opportunities for our teachers, and in the creation of new endowed chairs and institutes related to Orthodoxy and Hellenism. Included among them is the Mary Jaharis Institute for Byzantine Arts and Sciences at Hellenic College/Holy Cross, endowed with 3 million dollars, and the chair of New Testament Studies at Holy Cross, endowed with two million dollars. We have had, in addition, the Faith Endowment financial awards to the valedictorians and salutatorians of our day schools and of our communities, as well as to the finalists of the St. John Chrysostom Oratorical Festival.

4) The fourth development worth citing is the increase of our activities related to our Ecumenical Patriarchate of Constantinople, an increase due mostly to the commendable work of our Archdiocesan Archons of the Ecumenical Patriarchate, Order of Saint Andrew. These include: our professional assistance in the legal issues of our Patriarchate even to the point of substantial participation in the European Court of Human Rights in Strasbourg, France, last November. It is important to know that a week ago on July 8, 2008, the European Court of Human Rights vindicated our Ecumenical Patriarchate. Our activities further include the collection of signatures

of 80% of United States Senators in support of the rights of religious freedom of the Ecumenical Patriarchate, and the significant increase of our financial assistance to the Ecumenical Patriarchate to mention just a few.

5) The fifth noticeable item in this review is the growth of philanthropic activities in the past two years. Such growth is related to the commendable work of our Ladies Philoptochos Society. It is also related to extraordinary philanthropic activities like our assistance to the areas of Greece plagued last summer by devastating fires. The amount collected reached four million dollars, and the provided assistance followed a careful and systematic procedure responding to real needs detected by autopsy.

6) Allow me also to mention at this juncture three significant events outside of the United States in which our Church has had the great honor of participation. The first was the occasion of the historic visit by Pope Benedict XVI to our Ecumenical Patriarchate on November 2006, where as an Archdiocese we were invited, and where we offered a decisive organizational assistance in executing very demanding protocol at the highest level.

The second was our presence at the equally historic visit by our Ecumenical Patriarch Bartholomew to Rome, two weeks ago on the occasion of the Apostle Peter's thronic feast of the Roman Church. There, as a group of members of the Faith Endowment, we escorted our Patriarch and received with him an exceedingly honorific and cordial treatment by the Pope and his staff.

Then, the third significant event was our visit last May to the Patriarchate of Moscow. Invited by the Patriarch of Moscow, Patriarch Alexei, we were, as a group of twelve clergy and lay members of the Archdiocese, his guests for one week in Moscow. He treated us in an impressively cordial way, showing his appreciation and high esteem for what we are and for what we do in the United States and in the service of the Ecumenical Patriarchate, promoting cooperation and unity among Orthodox.

7) I would like also to make a reference to a very touching event of last year, namely to our strong support for the Archbishop of Athens and All Greece Christodoulos of blessed memory in the course of his heroic fight against cancer. Especially during the time from August to October 2007 of his staying in Miami, Florida, while he was waiting for the proper liver transplant, members of our Church were there and offered to the Archbishop and his escorts an astonishing assistance in kindness and effectiveness on a continuous, twenty-four hour basis.

8) I feel compelled to mention one more item of the last two years because it relates to our children and shows what wonderful voices children can be in calling people to God's Home, even outside of the United States. I am referring to the Children's Metropolitan Choir of our Archdiocese, comprised of 60 to 70 children of our Schools in the New York area. This choir, which has only been in existence for five years, demonstrated such artistic maturity in so short a time that it was invited last summer to Cyprus by the First Lady of Cyprus to give a

public concert in the Presidential Palace for the benefit of an institution for the children of working mothers called "Mana." The concert was an enormous success.

Two weeks ago, on July 3, the same Choir of children, thanks to the generosity of two of our blessed people who covered all the travel expenses, presented in Athens, Greece, another extremely successful public concert for the benefit of the Foundation "Elpis" (Hope), a foundation for children suffering from various forms of cancer; and two days later it offered another public concert at the convention of AHEPA in Athens. We thank God for all the children of our Church, who in many ways offer a convincing witness of our Faith.

For all these and many other signs of vitality and growth within our Holy Archdiocese which the limited time does not allow me to include at this moment, we profoundly thank God, who is our unfailing strength and guiding light.

Now, let us proceed to a series of comments and thoughts on the theme of our Congress, "Gather My People To My Home."

3. The theme of our Congress in the context of the contemporary religious landscape

1) The theme of the present 39th Biennial Clergy-Laity Congress of our Holy Archdiocese of America provides us with more than a slogan for our gathering. It constitutes a summons, a divinely-spoken directive that

we are called to follow in view of where we come from, what we are, and where we are destined by God to go.

For years we have been organizing our communities, providing educational, worshipping, and philanthropic opportunities for our members, building beautiful Churches, Community Centers and Schools for our own use.

This has been a natural course to follow as we tried to assert ourselves and to establish ourselves firmly as a significant entity and agent within the American society.

The Greek Orthodox Community in its first years of existence, in its first generation, was a community with a hundred percent participation of all of its members in the various activities of the Church. From the youngest child in a parish to its oldest member, people were always present as whole families in liturgical, educational and philanthropic events of the Church. The Church in the specific form of the parish, was the natural center where the community would gather, especially during the very difficult years of adaptation and survival in the new country where the heroic first immigrants, the true pioneers, found themselves.

2) With the passing of the years and the appearance of the second generation, the third, the fourth and now even the fifth generation, things gradually started to change. A new reality began to emerge, having the following characteristics:

a) First, in spite of the continuous, but in recent years more limited, phenomenon of immigration, our Church is by no means any longer a Church of immigrants, or an ecclesiastical entity of the diaspora, but a Church which is naturally, firmly and proudly rooted in the American soil. This means that the Church in our days is no longer preoccupied with the issue of the socio-economic survival of its immigrant members in a new country. Clearly, new conditions have been created. A recent statistic from the *U.S. Religious Landscape Survey*, produced by the Pew Forum on Religion and Public Life, shows that today approximately 45% of the members of our Community have at least one College degree, and also 45% have an annual income of or above $100,000, and that in both cases we are second among the major religious communities in the United States including Roman Catholics, Protestants and Jews. Having reached a level beyond that of socio-economic survival or even success, enjoying a freedom from pressing socio-economic concerns, the Church now is in a position to focus completely and intensely on promoting the Orthodox Faith and in cultivating the universal human values of Hellenism operative today in all civilized societies and countries.

b) Secondly, there exists no longer a full homogeneity in our Communities, the way it existed among the first immigrant communities. Today there is a certain difference between first generation immigrants and fifth generation Greek Americans. Also, the constantly increasing number of interfaith marriages has caused a change in the composition of the membership of the Church. A typical, well organized parish of our Metropolises presents an internal differentiation because of the difference in terms of levels of generations from first to fifth and of ethnic and even religious origin of several of its members.

c) Thirdly, in the present new reality of the Church, there is a serious problem with the youth. A certain number of high school adolescents, college and university students, and young adults, which means the people from 16 to 35 years of age, are somehow disconnecting themselves from the Church and Her life. This is a phenomenon occurring in all major religious Communities in the USA, but its general character does not diminish the fact that it constitutes a sad phenomenon, a major problem, and a grave concern for us.

d) Fourthly, there is a new reality in the religious landscape of contemporary America. This is the existence of the 60 million people characterized as "unchurched." These people are not atheists at all. They are individuals who for various reasons are not connected with any Church or organized religious body. Many were connected but at some point left their religious community. Others were never related to any religious body at all.

The above observations help us understand the importance of the theme of the present Congress: "Gather My People to My Home." We are no longer a Church community looking for survival. Such an understanding of ourselves belongs to the past. We cannot be a self-centered, self-enclosed Greek Orthodox ecclesiastical body, limited to itself and directing its energy exclusively within itself. We cannot be a ghetto Church. God calls us to gather His people. In order to gather God's people we have to go out, to look for them, to search places and find them and lead them to God's home. The theme of the Congress calls us in no uncertain terms to reach out, to move out and start gathering the souls who look for a spiritual home, for a living community and ultimately for a communion with God. How can we respond to such a sacred call?

Our response starts with a question: Who are the specific people to whom God sends us to gather them and to share with them the treasures of a life-giving faith?

4. Who are God's people whom we must gather to His Home?

1) First, they are our Orthodox brothers and sisters, members of our families, who were baptized, and perhaps even married in the Church, but are no longer strongly connected with Her. We see them on Palm Sunday, on Good Friday, and on the night of the Resurrection Service. There are thousands, even tens of thousands of them. Where are these people during the rest of the year? Obviously they are not connected or their connection is simply loose. We have to go out and invite and gather them and not wait for them to come once or twice a year, or on the sad occasion of a funeral in their family.

Looking for them should be a priority in each parish, aiming at systematically and tirelessly reaching out to our disconnected or very loosely connected Orthodox brothers and sisters who demographically belong to the area of the parish.

2) There is a second category of people of God whom we must invite and gather to His Home: they are the members of the interfaith marriages who after their marriage have not been in touch with the Church or who did not even have an Orthodox wedding service and, therefore, are completely unknown to us. Reaching out to them, finding them, requires greater effort. Such a task is not easy due to many factors, one of them being the high mobility of the population. The parishes, however, provide a good basis of information, having at their disposal data by which we could eventually locate and find the interfaith families which are not in touch with the Church. We must find them, with the help of God, and bring them to God's home.

3) The third category of people whom God asks us to gather to His Home are our young people, our adolescents and young adults, who, in one way or another, have left the Church. One might argue that this should not have happened, that we could have prevented such a sad disconnection. But it happened; it is a general phenomenon with every religion in America, and now we have to address the issue of gathering the disconnected young people to God's home, instead of passively complaining about the phenomenon.

Gathering them presupposes offering to them opportunities of learning the truth of the Gospel in a substantive and satisfactory way, relevant to the contemporary intellectual and social reality but also to the universal and eternal quest for God and to the ultimate meaning of life.

4) The fourth category are the "unchurched," the spiritually homeless. As we pointed out earlier, according to statistics there are today in the United States approximately 60 million unchurched. This is a category which is not located in a specific area or in a precise social group. They are dispersed everywhere: in the colleges and universities, in the working places, in the neighborhoods, in the airplanes and the cars, in Washington and New York, in Chicago and San Francisco, in Boston and Pittsburgh, in Atlanta and New Jersey, in Denver and Detroit. Reaching them is a very sensitive task because our Orthodox Church has always avoided engaging in the proselytizing of religious propaganda. We are not for proselytizing but for sharing what God gave us. Gathering the "unchurched" by sharing truth and love with them, and gathering them to God's home is a demanding task. But we must undertake it. This is a call by God, Who as St. Paul said to Timothy, *desires all people to be saved and to come to the knowledge of the truth:* ὅς πάντας ἀνθρώπους θέλει σωθῆναι καὶ εἰς ἐπίγνωσιν ἀληθείας ἐλθεῖν (1 Timothy 2:4).

5. The theme of our Congress as applied in the life of our Church.

Let me now, in the last part of my presentation, offer some suggestions aiming at applying the theme "Gather My People to My Home" to the life of the Church.

1) Any effort for a serious application of our theme must begin with a changing of mentality and attitude. We must change from an exclusive and all-absorbing focusing on our parish to an awareness of the existence of people outside of our Parishes, Metropolises and Archdiocese. People have the right to know what we know as the truth of God, to taste the joy of participating in our ecclesial community, and to experience the blessings we experience to be with God as we are by being Greek Orthodox Christians. The area of our focused action should gradually be enlarged by including those who are outside, by being concerned with those who are waiting for the brother or the sister who will bring them home. Offering the shelter of God to the homeless souls should be part of the care and action of our parishes, should be an indispensable part of our mentality, attitude and vision, and also should definitely be a central item of the basic education cultivated by the Church.

2) Each parish must appoint a committee which will have the duty of creating a list of the Greek Orthodox people who are residents of its parochial territory and are not connected with the Church. As soon as the names start being collected, the committee under the guidance of the priest will organize the ways of contact by using personal visits, phone calls, e-mail, church events, and distribution of the appropriate printed or electronic material. The parish could take advantage of its annual festival as an excellent opportunity to reconnect the people with the Church.

3) Another permanent committee should be instituted at each parish dealing exclusively with the non-connected interfaith marriage families. The committee, using the pertinent data existing in the parish, will find those families and bring them to God's home, the Church. Some of our parishes have a special program of introduction to Orthodoxy and to the universal human and cultural values of Hellenism, which show that our Church is not a limited and exclusive ethnic entity but a very inclusive and truly universal Home of God.

4) As Church, we have to review and reorganize our work in order to gather our youth home. Gathering the youth presupposes offering them a real role in the life of the community and further opportunities for meaningful activities. For young people at a certain age, athletic and artistic activities have been proven to be successful means of connecting them to community. Athletic tournaments, Folk Dance Festivals, and local Metropolitan Olympics have been truly successful youth activities.

In recent years we have seen the beginning of a successful reaching out to gather to God's home our university students by means of the OCF, the Orthodox Christian Fellowship. Today, by the grace of God, we have 270 OCF groups in an equal number of colleges and universities, a number steadily increasing. This is a work worth intensifying.

In reaching out for the youth and keeping them gathered to the home of God, the summer camps also offer a terrific opportunity. In our Metropolises, summer camps are now a basic and rapidly expanding activity involving hundreds of young people as leaders, advisors and campers. This might become an even more important and effective activity as it expands beyond the period of summer. In the case of the Ionian Village camp in Greece, we are currently exploring the possibility of expanding the programs to include not only children and adolescents but also young professional and university students on a year round basis.

5) The application of the theme "Gather My People to My Home" to the category of the "unchurched" constitutes a case that requires special care and action.

We can invite the unchurched, whom in one way or another we encounter, to our Church. But then we must be ready to welcome them, to be cordial and understanding, willing to share information and answer questions but not in a propagandistic way. The Orthodox Church is appreciated by other Christian Churches as a Church with a very kind human face and attitude and an aversion for religious propaganda, which is very different from lovingly sharing the truth of the Gospel. We reach out to the unchurched by starting today praying for them, for those who are unknown to us, but who are known to God as His children.

An interdepartmental committee will be formed in conjunction with the Archdiocesan Council for a serious study of the phenomenon of the unchurched and the ways to work effectively with them. The literature on the issue is increasing. Books like *Surprising Insights from the Unchurched and Proven Ways to Reach Them* or *The Unchurched Next Door* (T.S. Rainer) are indicative of the interest about the "unchurched" and the necessity of facing this issue methodically and persistently.

6) The effort of gathering the people of God to His home presupposes the availability of the proper and adequate resources, in the forms of books, DVDs, CDs and printed material. Our departments of Religious Education, Greek Education, Outreach and Evangelism, and Communications, which have been producing relevant material, are directed to intensify and enhance such a production and provide our Metropolises and our Parishes with necessary tools.

6. Epilogue

Certainly the task of applying the theme of our Congress to the life of our Church is not easy. And it becomes even more difficult by the spreading of secularism within contemporary societies. In recent studies, however, produced by political and social analysts and historians, it has been demonstrated that during the last four or five years two mighty factors unexpectedly emerged internationally: religion and ethnicity. Paradoxically, secularism is today confronted by the formidable and dominant presence of religion and ethnicity on a global scale. This phenomenon constitutes an important facilitation of our task to gather the people to the home of God, since we have the great gift of representing our Orthodox Christianity as the perfect religion and our Hellenic tradition as the amazing expression of an ethnicity which transcends its ethnic boundaries and becomes universal.

But beyond that, we have a very inspiring and highly motivating directive in one of the parables of our Lord Jesus Christ, which is an illustration of the substance of the theme of our Congress "Gather My People to My Home." This is the parable of the Great Banquet, from the Gospel according to St. Luke.

A certain man, said the Lord in this parable, gave a great banquet and invited many. The invited people, however, citing various reasons, excused themselves.

Then the householder said to his servant: "Go out quickly to the streets and lanes of the city and bring in the poor and maimed and blind and lame." And the servant said, "Sir, what you commanded has been done, and still there is room." And the master said to the servant, "Go out to the highways and hedges, and compel people to come in, that my house may be filled" (Luke 14:21-23).

The list of the invited people is striking, almost unbelievable: poor, maimed, blind, lame, gathered from the streets and lanes of the city and even from the highways and hedges! And they are not simply brought in but even compelled to come in. No discrimination, no differentiation, no exclusion, but the unknown, the despised and the strangers are all invited! A human field is presented, wide open, with no limits.

The important item here is not only the amazing list but the desire of the householder to have his house filled with all the people. The householder of the parable is unmistakably representing God. God wants His home to be filled with the people because all people on earth are His people. And we are part of His desire and plan, which simply means that we have to go literally out to the streets and lanes of the cities and to the highways and hedges and gather the people to the House of God, so that His House be filled.

There is one more statement that comes from the mouth of the Lord and is relevant to the theme of our Congress. In the Gospel of John, Christ declared: *"I have other sheep, that are not of this fold; and I must bring them also and they will hear my voice; and there shall be one flock one shepherd"* (John 10:16).

Jesus Christ speaks about other sheep that are not of this fold, but He has to bring them also. And they will hear His voice. Who are these other sheep that are not of this fold? And how are they going to hear Christ's voice?

Every time that we are in our churches, in our beautiful parishes, let us think of those other sheep, those other people who are outside, known and unknown, the ones described in the parable of the Great Banquet. Let us think of all others, the truly significant others, who wait to hear the voice of Christ. The voice of Christ invites them to gather in His home, to become His flock. But how can they hear the voice of Christ? W e   a r e   t h e   v o i c e   o f   C h r i s t ! My beloved people, let such a voice be heard outside of our Churches, calling the people of God to His home. L e t   u s   b e   t h e   v o i c e   o f   C h r i s t , everywhere, for everyone, at any time, at any place of the wide-world of God.

Universal Values of Religions

*Address for the
International Symposium at the Academy of Athens
On Universal Values*

May 26, 2004

1. I express my deep thanks to our President of the Academy of Athens and to the organizing committee for the invitation to speak this afternoon on the topic *Universal Values of Religions* before this august gathering of scholars from around the world. How fitting and relevant is this symposium on Universal Values, offered on the occasion of the Olympic Games and their return to their homeland! As we watch the whole world gather in Athens to applaud excellence in athletic achievement, we rightly take time to consider our common sense of excellence, our universal human values—εἴ τις ἀρετὴ καὶ εἴ τις ἔπαινος, if there is any excellence, if there is anything worthy of praise, in the words of the Apostle Paul (Philippians 4:8).

Before we proceed with the specific analysis and presentation of our topic, however, we might ask what the Olympic Games have to do with religious values. The answer is rather easy: much, in many ways. For the Games themselves gain their epithet from the fact that they were held in honor of Olympian Zeus, the supreme deity of the ancient Hellenic peoples. Whatever gods or goddesses the individual city-states may have honored in particular, they recognized the common religious values that were incorporated in the mythology of Olympian Zeus; and these things they celebrated through the displays of physical prowess that were the Olympic Games. It is fitting, therefore, that today, in conjunction with our own upcoming Olympic Games, we should pause to regard the universal values that are expressed in the variety of religious traditions which are represented by the athletes and spectators who make their way to Athens this summer. As you may have noticed, I have changed the original title "Universal Values and Religions" into "Universal Values of Religions." The intent is clear. The Religions of the world offer a tremendous amount of values that are truly universal and that could be considered genuine and full universal values.

2. One can hardly utter the phrase "universal religious values," however, without thinking of the saying of the ancient Hellenic poet, Xenophanes of Colophon, that each race of men depicts the nature and shapes of the gods as similar to its own. He says that the Ethiopians make their gods dark-skinned and broad of nose, whereas the Thracians depict them as red-haired and blue-eyed. And he adds that men also invent *souls* for the gods that are similar to their own, attributing to the gods, as Homer and Hesiod did, all human

properties and attributes, not only the good but even the bad ones.

On the face of it, the observation of Xenophanes, in spite of its simplicity, might be an argument that, in the realm of religious values, there is only *particularism* and *differentiation*. According to the Xenophanian observation, how can we speak of universal values, if every human theology seems to be a projection of each society's self-image into a heavenly setting? But that would be a rather naïve and superficial conclusion. Xenophanes himself did not surrender to agnosticism or atheism, even while holding himself in full awareness of the limitations of the religious sensibilities of his time and circumstances.

For our part, we would be remiss *not* to recognize that the religious sensibilities of humanity have evolved considerably since the time of Xenophanes, and with the subsequent worldwide expansion of the great monotheisms: Judaism, Christianity, and Islam. Were we to limit the scope of our discussion to the common values of the above three monotheistic faiths, very much indeed could be said about their shared sense of cosmology, of revelation, of anthropology, of eschatology, and of ethics.

This, however, would methodologically be wrong. It would be an evasion of our intellectual responsibility towards the members of the Academy and the participants in this symposium, which is a Symposium on *Universal* Values. And so, along with the monotheistic creeds, we must consider which values are common to them and to all other religions, such as Hinduism and Shintoism; as well as to the formally non-theistic religions, such as Buddhism, Confucianism, and Taoism; and, of course, to all forms of minor polytheistic religions espoused by isolated tribes in Africa and elsewhere.

Still, more must be said. Even this sweeping list of faiths from around the world does not constitute the basis for a survey of *universal* religious values. We must also include the sensibilities of the ancient folk religions and fertility cults, as exemplified by the familiar pantheon and piety of the Hellenic peoples; as well as the traditional animistic religions; and at the other end of the spectrum, the Gnostic sects that co-existed with early Christianity; and even the newer faiths and philosophies, such as the Bahai Faith and Mormonism. Setting this as our standard of universal inclusiveness then, moves the discussion quite far away from a mere comparative study of the three major monotheistic faiths—Judaism, Christianity and Islam—and the common set of values they have derived from one another.

3. Following such a methodological perspective we are not going to deal with well known general or humanistic universal values like peace, justice, freedom, brotherhood and human rights. These universal values might not be shared by all religions, as we unfortunately know from our human history. Therefore, the main question is: What values do all religions of humankind have in common which constitute true universal values of religions? In order to have the proper answer, we must look beyond the realm of specific dogmas, and instead

begin at the level of human experience, aiming at finding the genuine universal values shared by all religions.

  a. It is the common experience of human societies, throughout time and across the globe, that there is a Divine Someone, a Divine Something in this world, a Presence, a Power or Force that defies definition, measurement, or analysis. "How can we name Him who is beyond any possible name?" as St. Gregory the Theologian said. This Divine Presence is outside of the physics of the cosmos. It is the *ganz andere* ("wholly other") of Rudolph Otto's definition, and yet it is something that can be experienced by those in the natural world. It is a Force that acts upon the world, and that even *interacts* with humankind, yet it is not in the control of humans. Not every human being has a sense of this Divine Something, but every human community expresses somehow its experience of an encounter with this Divine Presence. In fact, one might define a "religion" as the response of a community to its encounter with this Divine Presence, no matter how vague or even imperceptible this presence is.

  Different human communities respond to different elements of their encounter. The great Asian religious traditions tend to emphasize the ways in which the universe is held in equilibrium by this Divine Power; and so they cherish especially ideas of balance, harmony, and poetic justice, as are evoked by terms like *yin* and *yang*, or *karma*. In folk religions, the encounter is construed more in terms of how the presence of the Divine brings about life and growth in the natural world, leading to development of the symbols of fertility which, under various guises, find their way into every religious tradition. In the great Western traditions, this Divine Presence is encountered more in terms of how it inspires the ethical life of humankind, and consequently there has been significant development of religious thought in terms such as righteousness and holiness, good versus evil. In nearly every religious tradition, this encounter is prized for the measure of healing that it brings, both in terms of well-being for the body and inner peace for the heart and mind of man.

But this encounter is not itself so much a "universal value." It is rather an artist's palette from which the various religious communities have drawn their own particular expressions of their experiences, each according to the tints and hues of a given viewpoint and perspective, with the canvas being the evolving traditions of each community. But in examining the various canvasses of faith, one does find a considerable common core of values to consider.

b. The first great universal religious value is *reverence*. The substance of this universal religious value of reverence is interesting, and from a certain point of view, perhaps even a little unexpected. Reverence is not easily defined; we know it when we see it, but it is difficult to find words that fully express the condition of the human heart in a state of reverence. The best place to start may be with the statement of the American philosopher Paul

Woodruff in his work on reverence, which he regards as "the well-developed capacity to have the feelings of awe, respect, and shame when these are the right feelings to have."[1] Reverence, then, is the ability to maintain an appropriate self-consciousness, one that combines a sense of limitedness and even, in moments of awe, a sense of personal smallness *vis-à-vis* the Divine Presence.

In the face of the encounter with the Divine Presence, with the Wholly Other, humans rightly respond with reverence. The concrete objects of reverence vary from tradition to tradition; for some it is icons, for others sacred texts, and for others elements of the natural world. The crucial feature of reverence, however, is not so much the external objects towards which it is consciously directed, as it is the human personality to which it is attached. Every religious tradition, it seems, makes the distinction between reverent and irreverent persons, between the pious and the impious. The great Homeric epics of the Hellenic peoples can be analyzed as being grand cautionary tales on the rewards of reverence and the consequences of irreverence, and the pragmatic need to make the distinction in dealing with one's fellow human beings. This is not the same as the distinction between believer and non-believer, for every tradition seems to acknowledge the existence of externally religious people who lack the internal qualities that are consistent with the tenets of faith.

[1]Paul Woodruff, *Reverence: Renewing a Forgotten Virtue* (Oxford: Oxford University Press, 2001).

Every religious tradition has as a key value, some notion of reverence, although in outward terms this virtue is expressed in vastly different ways: to Christians in the Orthodox tradition, the custom of venerating sacred objects and people with a bow and a kiss is an age-old expression of reverence; but to Christians from Western traditions, this action can be seen in a different light; and yet, as different as the expressions of reverence are, the web of feelings and attitudes connected with it bear a striking similarity across religious traditions. Likewise, every tradition has, in opposition to the value of reverence, the corresponding vice, which is called in its original Greek term ὕβρις, *hubris,* which is in its essence an inability to feel awe, respect, or shame in any encounter with the Divine Presence. It took the so-called "Age of Reason"—which is at bottom simply a decline of religious sensibility, and not any great increase in the exercise of rationality—to elevate hubris from vice to virtue in the eyes of the common man. The idealized models of the successful businessman or politician or athlete nowadays project a psychological makeup characterized by the mentality of a lack of limitations, an absence of awe. The universal religious value of reverence, therefore, is at odds with the post-modern paradigms of easy and naïve fulfilled personhood, and may very well act as a counterbalancing agent to the unhealthy anthropocentric autonomy of various humanisms.

c. This consideration leads us to the next universal value of religions, which is *the battle against the dark force* of irreverence that opposes the Divine Presence and Divine operation within the world. Common to all religious traditions is the sense that this opposing force is characterized by a sense of unfounded irreverence, of delusion or hubris or deception: it is a spirit of contradiction. In the Western traditions this contrary force is epitomized in the person of Satan; in Eastern religion it is the deceptiveness of *maya*, "illusion," the sense of reality that the world holds over human consciousness. In every case, it is the failure of reverence, the deceitfulness of hubris, that brings about the principle of opposition.

Thus, one of the corollary universal values of religions is the sense of tension, even struggle or battle, between the Wholly Different, the mystery that nurtures the world, which mystery is the ultimate cause and object of all human reverence, and its opposing principle. From this tension, the entire drama of world history evolves. Common also to all religious value systems is the idea that the human race and its members individually play some role in the cosmic contest. Ours is not simply another species of mammals populating this planet. Religious faith the world over has detected a crucial role for humanity in the struggle, through the exercise of human choice, to either align with the side of the mystery of the Divine Presence and Power that nurtures, or with the force that negates. To borrow the terminology of western religion, humankind has an important role in battling with God in overcoming the opposing powers of darkness and destruction. It is clear that the cosmic tension involves a considerable degree of human cooperation and participation.

Religion, then, universally holds two corresponding values concerning the human condition, namely, the value of reverence towards the Divine Presence and the value of participating in the battle against the dark force opposing the Divine Presence in the universe.

d. From these more metaphysical values of worldwide religions, a number of other values arise, of particular anthropological interest. There is, as a universal feature of religions, *a sense of blessing*. That is to say, a perception that human beings, as part of their role in the cosmic contest, have an ability to convey somehow the mysterious Divine Power or Presence to the world which they inhabit. This blessing can be performed through sacred gestures or simple rituals, or through the lengthy prayers of Eucharist found in the Orthodox Christian traditions. This idea of blessing, by whatever means, is central to every religious value system: it is the point of contact between visible nature and the invisible; or rather, it is the means by which the blending of the immanent and the transcendent takes place, working ultimately to a resolution of the cosmic contest.

Not every religious system has a distinction between clergy and laity as a standing bifurcation of the society into permanent and separate roles in the act of blessing. Nor does every religion have a fixed sense of sacred space, such as in temples and houses of worship; or of sacred time, as in a calendar of feasts and festivals.

Thus, the act of blessing may be a very private and provisional one, or it may be a very public and permanent one, as when a Christian congregation consecrates a new edifice as a church. In either case, the fundamental value persists—that the free choice of human beings, engaged in appropriate actions in a reverential spirit, can cooperate with the mysterious and nurturing Divine Presence in the world with the effect of creating a blessing upon the people or upon some element of the created order.

e. Concomitant with the value of blessing, there is a universal property of religions to have an activity which one can label as *prayer*. Prayer here is not to be conceived only as a basic religious phenomenon, or merely as an act of supplication to a personal deity, or even as a more generalized event of communication at the semantic level. Prayer is rather an exercise of the human faculty of speech for the purpose of opening up the entire human person for an encounter with the transcendent and nurturing Presence of God. The capacity for verbal communication is widely held as the key faculty differentiating humans from other animals, and as such in the religions of the world it is invested with a unique potential for sacred work.

By prayer is meant something different from the idea of a verbal blessing. The words of prayer, whether fixed or free, whether many or few, whether replete with semantic content or devoid thereof, are primarily a ground upon which an encounter with the transcendent Significant Other, with the great mystery of life, takes place. Nothing in this natural world has to change for prayer to be effective; the best prayer is not necessarily the one that procures the desires of one's heart, but rather the one that instills in the person who is praying, the correct desires to have in the heart. Prayer is ultimately an act of sacrifice greater than any burnt offering or financial donation. True prayer is an offering up of the one and only thing that we humans truly have of our own to give away: our will. Prayer is the verbal gift of our choice to the ways of the Ultimate Other, of God. Thus, it constitutes a universal value of tremendous importance for the entirety of humanity in any time and any place.

  f. For this reason, religious communities cherish the modes of prayer that are effective in fostering the encounter with the nurturing mystery of faith. This leads to the next universal value of religions, the value of *memory*. Every religious tradition takes pains to safeguard the communal memory of the tradition. For the people of the Book—Jews, Christians, and Muslims—this value of memory is encoded in graphic symbols of faith. For other traditions, the memory is encoded in a system of practices, designed to preserve and honor the contributions of those who have gone before. It is no accident that the learning of the ancient world survived the so-called Dark Ages of Western Europe in the monasteries, for "Thou shalt preserve the memory" is the unwritten commandment of religious communities the world over. This universal value of memory offered today by all religions is of vital importance. Our modern world very easily tends to forget; it limits itself to a suffocating present and uncertain future. Memory brings liberation and opens amazing perspectives.

    g. This leads to one of the most striking universal values of religions, a value of diachronic quality. This is the value of *music*. One could profitably speak for hours about the place of the arts in general in religious traditions, but there is truly only one art form that rises to the level of a value in every form of human religious expression, and that is music.

In light of what has been mentioned already, the role of music in the religious encounter becomes clear. Music is pre-eminently an aid to memory, a means for preserving a community's legacy of faith in a form that can be recollected and passed down, with or without the gift of writing. Music is for many humans the truest form of prayer, a means by which they transcend the mere communication of needs and wishes and advance to a plane of openness to an encounter with the divine. Music in the form of chanting is a most natural way for an event of blessing to be conveyed. Music has a power to inspire human beings like few other things in the world, and in fact, music is often conceived of as being something not quite of this world, but as a gift from heaven, an imitation of life in a higher celestial sphere, and special bequest of the nurturing mystery of life.

    Music has the power to kindle love in the heart, and for this reason it stands as one of the few truly universal religious values. For it is related to the one core religious value of all peoples: the value of love. Little need be said about love, for we all understand what love is, even if we cannot define it.

4. We have seen in an extremely condensed way some of the universal values of religion: We started with the value of reverence in view of our encounter with the Divine Being. Then, we proceeded with the reality of the powers opposing the Divine Presence in the world, and the value of fighting against them. Next, we studied the universal value of religions in the sense of blessing that we carry as human beings connected with the Divine Power. Prayer is another universal value offered by the religions of the world. We discussed briefly another important universal religious value, which is the memory, and we ended with the most amazing universal religious value, i.e. music.

The pertinent list could continue *ad infinitum*. But we stop here at an open-ended point that invites further thought and serious consideration. Of course, we do not need to show how the universal values of religions presented above relate to the universal values in general. We could simply say that the universal values of religions are universal values today, as they were in the past, and as they will be in the future.

A Christian Spirituality of Peace and Justice in a Violent World

*Keynote Address
International Conference on Violence
and Christian Spirituality*

*Hellenic College/Holy Cross School of Theology
October 27, 2005*

1. Introduction

The presence and threat of violence in our contemporary world is very real and challenging. Daily we are confronted with means and types of death and destruction that seem unfathomable. We are challenged to address the effects and consequences of violence upon our neighbors, our communities, our nations and our world. At the same time, our physical, mental, and spiritual well-being is challenged by a violent world in a very deep and formative way.

What is the relationship of our Christian faith to the violence we see in the world? How do we respond to violence in a manner that is rooted in our faith and our relationship with God? In this relationship with a God of peace and justice, how do we experience peace and justice in our own lives and labor for the same in the lives of others, in our communities, and in our world?

In order to answer these difficult questions, we as Christians and Churches in a violent world, must understand the significance of our spirituality of peace and justice. We must examine carefully the foundations of a Christian spirituality of peace and justice as revealed to us by Christ and through the witness of the great Saints, Teachers, and Martyrs of the Church. By looking to the foundation of our faith we can know the true definition of peace and justice, the significance of peace and justice for our lives, relationships, and hopes, and how peace and justice are offered to our world. This is an essential place to begin in examining any relationship between Christian spirituality and violence.

And let us begin by first examining the issue of,

2. Peace and Justice in the Teachings and Ministry of Christ

Blessed are the peacemakers, for they will be called the children of God. Blessed are those who are persecuted for righteousness' sake, for theirs is the kingdom of heaven (Matthew 5:9-10).

In these words from the Sermon on the Mount, our Lord Jesus Christ affirmed that peace is essential to our relationship with God. If we are to be known as His children, we will receive a true and enduring peace from Him, a peace that comes from the transformation of our souls, hearts, and minds in His image and will. We will also share this peace with others. To become His children means that we become peacemakers ($εἰρηνοποιοί$).

But the words of Christ are also a recognition of the reality of our world. Evil and sin have brought violence and death into a realm that was created for peace and life. In this fallen world, violence is so prevalent that even for those who seek and do what is right and just, the response will often be persecution. But Christ calls the peacemakers and the righteous "blessed." He associates them with God in a familial way, acknowledging that the inheritance of the kingdom is theirs.

To know the significance of this blessing upon "the peacemakers," we must first understand the nature of the peace that comes from God and is revealed to us in Christ. Let us remember the magnificent revelation of the love of God in the Incarnation. Christ entered into our human existence and the world to reveal to us true peace, and, in the words of Zechariah the father of John the Baptist and Forerunner, *to guide our feet into the way of peace* (Luke 1:79). On the night of His birth, the angels appeared to the shepherds and announced, *Glory to God in the highest, and on earth peace, goodwill among men* (Luke 2:14). His life and ministry were characterized by the peace He revealed and the peace that He brought to the lives of others. For those who were seeking God, the truth He preached fostered peace, His healing touch restored peace, and His divine presence assured them of an enduring peace that would abide in their hearts forever. It was this peace that was given to His disciples on the night of the Last Supper before they saw the man of peace suffer and die so violently. *Peace I leave with you; my peace I give to you* (John 14:27).

In the actions and words of Christ it is evident that the peace of God is the gift and blessing of the grace of God and His love for humankind. It is a peace that comes from the assurances of a divine and compassionate presence, a peace that offers a level of security and joy that can come from no other source in heaven or on earth. But how, some may ask, does this peace exist in a violent world? How can someone find peace when the threat of violence is imminent? Again, we look to Christ who experienced the violence of our world. He was unjustly wounded, bruised, and crushed for our sake. But even though He was the recipient of terrible acts of violence, He knew that this violence, rooted in sin, ignorance, and the rejection of God, would not triumph, and that its defeat would not come through even greater acts of violence. Victory would come through a sacrificial act of love on the part of God for the salvation of all humanity. Therefore, even though Christ experienced enormous suffering, the peace of God that rested upon Him came from a much greater spiritual source of life that would break the bonds of sin and death and bring about His physical Resurrection. This is why in the Orthodox Church we refer to the Cross of Christ as a "weapon of peace." It is this power of sacrifice and love, not violence, that defeats sin and death and brings hope and peace to our souls. It is also this act and example of Christ that restores our relationships with God and one another, and reveals that through love, true peace can exist in a violent world.

It is also this same principle and experience of the love of God that helps us to define a Christian spirituality of justice in a violent world. It is in our relationship with God through Christ that we know what is just, that we are guided in the path of holiness, and that we seek to be the righteous ones who will inherit the Kingdom of God. Further, as we are reconciled to God by His grace, we know that this reconciliation is offered to all people. In Colossians 1:19-20, Saint Paul states, *For in him all the fullness of God was pleased to dwell, and through him God was pleased to reconcile to himself all things, whether on earth or in heaven, by making peace through the blood of his Cross.* As Christians, our understanding of justice is not a forceful or violent condemnation of our world and our fellow human beings. Ours is a justice of compassion that seeks to reconcile each and every person to God by means of the transforming love he has revealed to us. We will not sit upon the throne of Judgment, but Christ alone; and how will we be judged? As we well know, according to Christ, it will be upon the measure of how we respond in compassion to the needs of others. *Come, you that are blessed by my Father, inherit the kingdom prepared for you from the foundation of the world; for I was hungry and you gave me food, I was thirsty and you gave me something to drink, I was a stranger and you welcomed me, I was naked and you gave me clothing, I was sick and you took care of me, I was in prison and you visited me* (Matthew 25:34-36).

This justice of compassion is our ministry and work in this world. It is also our basis from which we as Christians address the injustices that are not only the result of physical violence, but also violence that is done in the name of progress when human beings are marginalized, deemed expendable or of no value, or deprived of the basic necessities and blessings of life because of political or economic agendas. This was the message and ministry of Christ who came in peace and responded to the spiritual and physical needs of humankind, and it is through our life in Him that we know and experience a spirituality of peace and justice.

Let us now proceed with briefly presenting a second issue, namely

3. The Spirituality of Peace and Justice in the Early Church

The ministry and teachings of Christ guided the early Christians, who responded in the peace of God and in a justice of compassion to the needs of others even under the threat of violence. It is this example provided to us by these early believers that affirms the scriptural theme for this conference. Writing to the Christians at Philippi about the nature and goal of the Christian life, Paul states, *"keep on doing the things that you have learned and received and heard and seen in me, and the God of peace will be with you"* (Philippians 4:9). What is the spiritual orientation that is blessed by the peace of God? As Paul indicates, the peace of God rests upon those who seek *whatever is true, whatever is honorable, whatever is just, whatever is pure, whatever is pleasing, and whatever is commendable* (Philippians 4:8). In the midst of struggle, persecution, imprisonment, and the threat of violence, the early Christian communities were led by the example of Christ and the teaching of the Apostles to keep their hearts and minds on the truth, honor, justice, and purity that characterizes those who are reconciled to God and thus living in His kingdom. The focus here was upon the eternal nature of life in the kingdom of God in contrast to the temporal nature of the sufferings of this world. Christians were called to find peace and hope in the knowledge that nothing in heaven or on earth could separate them from the love of God and from the gift of life He offered.

This understanding of life and of true peace and justice did not lead the early Christians to forsake the world. In fact, as stated above, it guided them in a ministry of reconciliation. It revealed to them the true and enduring source of power that offered and sustained life, rather than controlling, manipulating and abusing it for the sake of material gain. It strengthened them so that they could stand and offer a witness of faith in the face of adversity, persecution, and even physical death.

It is here that we should direct our attention to two examples from the New Testament that show us the basic characteristics of a Christian spirituality of peace and justice. The first is that of Saint Stephen the First Martyr. What we find in this account of the trial and martyrdom of Stephen, is a young and spirit-filled believer who, under the threat of death, responded in a way that speaks to us today about our ministry of peace and justice in a violent world. First, Saint Stephen boldly addressed the council in the power of wisdom and truth. He was not afraid of the violence that might result from those who would take offence at his annunciation of the truth; for while he spoke clearly of the revelation of God's love, he firmly condemned the unjust treatment of Jesus Christ. Second, his actions revealed a deep faith in the providence of God. He placed his life, well-being, and future in the care of God and in His divine will, and was thus given a vision of heaven, the glory of God, and Jesus standing at the right hand of God (Acts 7:54). Third, his faith in God and in His promises nurtured within him compassion and forgiveness toward those who treated him unjustly. As Christ had done on the Cross toward those who crucified him, Stephen asked God to forgive those who acted violently out of their ignorance of the peace and will of God.

These principles of a Christian spirituality of peace and justice, exemplified by Saint Stephen and his martyrdom, are also evident in another story from the life of the early Church. After arriving in Philippi on their missionary journey, Paul and Silas were seized and brought before the magistrates. They were accused of violating the law, and they were attacked by the crowd, which stripped and beat them with rods. They were then thrown into prison. The response of Paul and Silas to these unjust acts of violence offers us further insights on the nature of a Christian spirituality of peace and justice. As with Saint Stephen, the Apostles Paul and Silas offered a witness of the presence of God. While chained in prison, they were praying and singing hymns to God.

Further, as a result of their faith, the power of God was made known in an earthquake that shook the foundations of the prison, opening prison doors and unfastening chains. They had trusted in His providence and promises, knowing that His will would be accomplished not by their use of violent means or by force, but through prayer and love. For these two Apostles, and for many others in the early Church and down through the centuries, the peace and love of God was so engraved upon their hearts and minds that no matter what the physical threat or condition, the response was one that did not answer violence with violence, but sought to transform lives and communities through the power of God's love.

In examining a Christian spirituality of peace and justice we could name countless other examples of those who in the face of violence revealed the peace of God and a justice of compassion. All of these are examples to us, the inheritors of the faith and the work and ministry of the Church that leads us in life and service in a violent world. How do we apply this example and this heritage of peace and justice in confronting violence in our contemporary world? How can we as Christians and Churches contribute to a culture of peace and justice that is so desperately needed to provide and sustain life and well-being?

Now, I am coming to the last part of my presentation, dealing with the issue of,

4. Confronting Violence with a Christian Spirituality of Peace and Justice

In our contemporary world violence must be confronted first and foremost by our witness of the presence of God in our lives and in communities of faith. This is our calling and witness in responding to the physical and spiritual needs of humanity; however, it is also our manner of life that reveals the true nature of peace and justice through our love and relationships. As the Church, we are called to model true community, offering to the world an example of how we live in peaceful and beneficial relationships with one another. As communities of faith, we continue to confront violence and its devastating effects with a ministry of compassion and hope, not condemning those who are the victims, but helping to secure the well-being of anyone in need. The transforming effects of this upon lives will foster a growing culture of peace and justice.

Second, we should follow the example of Christ and the Apostles by affirming the power and relevance of the Gospel to our contemporary world. In the person and message of Christ we find a true and timeless understanding of peace and justice that offers us strength in an environment of uncertainty, peace in the midst of upheaval, hope through extreme circumstances, and the assurance of life in the face of death. The examples of myriads of martyrs and great champions of our faith serve as very real examples of the powerful effects and witness our lives can have upon the world when we stand peacefully and honorably for what is true, just, and pure. The message of the Gospel is one that calls us on to a higher plane of being in communion with God and one another, a manner of life and existence that is lacking in cultures and communities that advocate violence as a means of power and domination. In the midst of an environment of turmoil and injustice we can offer a message of truth about the dignity of humankind and the power of love.

Third, in addition to our witness and ministry, we must direct in a cooperative and united manner the attention of our leaders and societies to the grave injustices of our world. Our spirituality of peace and justice must guide us in addressing societies, governments, and nations concerning the nature of human existence and the proper means for establishing peace and justice. This means that we must be willing to engage in challenging and sometimes unpopular deliberations regarding the communal use of force and, when this is appropriate, to maintain peace and secure justice against very dark and evil forces that can pose very serious regional and global threats to life, equality, and freedom.

This prophetic role of the Church, when rooted in a spirituality of peace and justice, will not be compromised by forms of radicalism that call for violence in the service of God. When the will of a gracious God is associated with violence, what results is a denial of our new nature in Christ, a detour from the path toward what is true, just, honorable, and pure. This does not prevent us from confronting the workings of sin and evil in our world; but in a very different way. The justification of violence will only lead to further and greater acts of violence. Therefore, our challenge is to use our resources and cooperation to build and strengthen institutions and programs of peace throughout the world. This should be done not in condemnation of others who may not share our faith, but in recognition of our common humanity and our God-given capacity to determine what is good and just and perfect (Romans 12:1).

As Churches and Christians we must be what we are called to be. Our understanding of peace and justice and labors for peace and justice offer the world a greater vision of human life and potential. We must shed light upon what is just, as well as upon what is not. The light of truth should shine into every place in the world, in our own homes and communities and in our dialog with world leaders, governments, and people of other faiths. A culture of peace and justice should truly be known. In addition, our spirituality of justice and peace should define all of our relationships both local and global. As the leaven in the bread, we know that the labor for peace and justice is one that is often very slow and challenging. Societal, cultural, and political structures that employ violence or that exist due to injustice are often so ingrained in the lives of people that they either know no other way of existence, or they are resigned to a subhuman manner of life. We must confront this. A true spirituality of peace and justice will be evident in a lifelong commitment to faith and worship, to the will of God, to the principles of His Kingdom, so that when violence comes, whether it be in the form of terrorism, economic collapse, natural disasters, environmental catastrophes, political unrest, war, or shortages of resources, the peace of God and a justice of compassion will guide us and our communities in a spirit of love and brotherhood that will affirm our faith in God and our trust in His providence and promises.

5. Conclusion

We have seen and experienced many violent acts over the past decade that have changed our world in a very dramatic and substantial way. How have we responded to violence as Christians? Has our response been rooted in our faith and our communion with God? Do we think about the threat of violence in these terms? Is our Christian faith viewed only as a place of solace following acts of violence, or are we discovering a renewal of hope and peace in the midst of uncertainty? The focus of our governments is on preparing for violence, either in forms of terrorism or natural disasters. Are we preparing spiritually? Are we reconnecting our communities with our spiritual heritage of peace and justice and consistently reaffirming it, so that believers are able to see the relevance of their spiritual lives in responding to violence and to living in a violent world? As leaders, teachers, theologians, clergy, and believers may we be committed to nurturing this spirituality of peace and justice among our communities and through them in our world; and in fulfilling this sacred vocation, may *the peace of God, which surpasses all understanding, guard your hearts and minds in Christ Jesus* (Philippians 4:7).

A Free Society Founded on Truth: Truth Making People Free

*Ninth Dialogue
between the Orthodox Church and
The Group of the European People's Party
(Christian Democrats) and European Democrats*

*October 20-21, 2005
Istanbul, Turkey*

I express my sincere thanks to the distinguished representatives of the Ecumenical Patriarchate and the European Parliament for the opportunity to address you this afternoon during what by now has become a well-established, internationally respected, and continuing dialogue. It is important that dialogues such as this continue to be active in years to come, particularly in the context of important themes that we are discussing, namely European Solidarity, Cooperation, and Enlargement.

In light of these themes, I wish to offer some thoughts about the important subject of truth as embodied by the very appropriate title of this session: "A Free Society founded on Truth – Truth Making People Free." This title is suggestive of the memorable and powerful statement uttered by Jesus to the people, *You will know the truth, and the truth will make you free* (John 8:32). Jesus' words, then as now, have profound existential and political value. First, they imply that truth is not a vague philosophical or abstract notion, but, rather, that truth is a living reality which is necessary for freedom. We are called to know the truth and live in truth in order to enjoy freedom as we relate to others through dialogue, as we worship God our Creator, and as we work toward authentic reconciliation of differences with one another. Second, Jesus' words imply that the way of diverse societies to commit themselves to ensuring civil liberties, religious freedom, and human rights is founded on truth which guarantees the establishment of true, all-encompassing freedom.

1. Dialogue as truth leading to freedom

Truth is not an abstract notion. It is a reality of life especially expressed in our relationships with others. How we relate to others accounts much for the question of how we live our lives in truth.

In the simplest of ways, our capacity to live in truth through our relationships with others is seen in the context of our day-to-day affairs. It is seen in our daily interactions with neighbors, co-workers, friends, persons known and also unknown.

In a more specific sense, our capacity to live in truth through our relationships with others is evidenced by our personal dialogues or by formal dialogues such as this. Here, in a dialogue like the present one, we see not a casual or informal human exchange, but a conscious, focused, and structured exchange of ideas and interactions directed toward very specific and measurable purposes. Accordingly, our capacity to live in truth as we relate to one another on heightened cognitive, intellectual, and spiritual levels is itself deepened. We become richer and more authentic human beings, and we reach new realms of freedom when we allow ourselves to engage in dialogue determined by truth.

As we consider dialogue in the context of European cooperation and enlargement, as we consider what it means to bring together people of diverse cultures, socio-economic conditions, religions, and historical backgrounds, we begin to capture the magnitude of our heightened potential as human beings to live authentically, to live in truth. This is because, through dialogue, we begin to gain knowledge of how others view the world, and how various historical and cultural dynamics have influenced others' perceptions and life experiences. Through our dialogue with others, we gain access to aspects of truth that liberate us from a narrow, limited understanding of the world, which is in essence a pluralistic world.

This reality of pluralism is one that does not diminish truth; on the contrary, it conveys, in an honest and representative manner, the totality of the human experience, which is necessary for a full adherence to the truth. In this regard, engaging in dialogue even with strangers is much like learning a new language, in that each party in dialogue is challenged to synthesize differing sets of foreign symbols, cultural references, literary allusions, and religious expressions. This exercise is intrinsic to knowing the truth of the human condition and to enjoying the freedom that such truth conveys. Dialogue is a way of accessing and experiencing truth that is vital to any meaningful and fruitful discussions about freedom, particularly in the context of European solidarity, cooperation, and enlargement.

2. Worship as liberating truth

As an existential personal condition, truth must pervade the totality of the human experience, not only in our relating to others, not only in our formal or informal dialogues, but particularly in our worship of God, the Creator of our universe and of all humankind. Here we have a tremendously important declaration by Jesus in His famous dialogue with the Samaritan woman, as vividly presented in the Gospel of John. Jesus said: *God is spirit, and those who worship Him must worship in spirit and truth* (John 4:24). The Lord makes it very clear here that the spiritual and truthful dimensions of worship are fundamental. It is impossible to offer authentic worship to God in the absence of spirit and truth. One cannot worship solely with the body; one cannot worship in falsehood. Those who worship God **must** worship *in spirit and truth*.

The consequence of worshipping in spirit and truth for human beings is genuine liberation and freedom for human beings, for by worship, man is able to satisfy his yearning to enter into a meaningful, living and substantive dialogue with his Creator. Such a dialogue is simply impossible if it is not based on truth and freedom, if it is not aiming at a full and genuine communication. For the purposes of our dialogue, I suggest that we should consider that we are coming together during these two days not simply to discuss important issues for Europe and indeed our world, but mainly to discuss them in a spirit of searching for the truth in these issues. Our personal dialogue then with God, being a dialogue of truth, helps us to establish the same attitude in the dialogues among us, an attitude of liberating truth. From that point of view, and because of the decisive impact that the dialogue with God in worship has on any other human dialogue, we must make every effort to guarantee and protect the freedom of worship for every human being. And this is a central task for the present meeting.

3. Reconciliation based on truth

The theme of reconciliation has received much attention in our times, as we can see it as the crucial theme in many interfaith and ecumenical gatherings that have taken place in different parts of the world, and which have been dedicated to this important topic. By reconciliation, we automatically imply two related concepts. First, by using the term "reconciliation" there is the automatic implication that at some point in time in history, arising from either a specific conflict or series of conflicts, there has been a breach in the state of peaceful relationship among the affected persons, societies or nations. Second, there is the automatic implication that the parties in conflict, both the injurer and the injured party, recognize at some level that the overcoming of such a breach and the enjoyment of the freedom that comes with reconciliation, may only be brought about through doing the difficult work that demands the courageous act of total commitment to the truth, because without truth there is no way to achieve lasting reconciliation.

Authentic reconciliation demands truth. Reconciliation necessitates the task of careful, probative, and prayerful research with the aim of finding the truth about the causes which lead to conflicts. Often, this task is threatening because it demands that we unveil shortcomings, misgivings, and wrongdoings that have been masked throughout history. It may also be threatening because it requires that we subject ourselves to those measures that are pursuant to justice. But the task of reconciliation is integrally related to the uncovering of truth in historical conflicts and controversies. Reconciliation is possible only by allowing the truth to be operative in interpersonal relationships, in relations among nations, and in the important work of dialogue among religions.

The notion that truth is something that can be covered up over the course of history, and that it subsequently needs to be uncovered through a conscientious process, constitutes a powerful statement about the human condition. It essentially implies that, left unchecked, our natural human tendency after the breach of a peaceful relationship is to gloss over the painful or controversial episodes of history that caused that breach. Perhaps this tendency arises out of the superficial belief that, over time, such episodes may be forgotten by both the injurer and those who are injured. Thus, the difficult work of reconciliation is centered around uncovering the truth, the truth that liberates.

St. Paul in his Second Epistle to the Corinthians (5:11-19) describes reconciliation in its absolute application, namely as the restoration of the broken relationship between God and humanity, as an ultimate act by God *who through Christ reconciled Himself to us and gave us the ministry of reconciliation.* In this regard, we may view reconciliation not as a human enterprise, but as a divine undertaking initiated by our Creator and given to human beings as an example of healing, freedom, and truth. Thus, when we participate in reconciliation, we engage in an act of imitating God, Who is the Reconciler in truth and freedom.

4. Civil liberties based on truth

So far, we have been discussing the liberating function of truth as expressed in dialogue, worship, and reconciliation. These aspects are essential for living authentically as human beings in relationship with others and with God. Yet there are also aspects of truth that are intrinsically political; that is, aspects related to the institutional structures, workings, and integrity of a free, well-organized society. The first of these aspects refers to the issue of civil liberties.

Civil liberties encompass a wide range of fundamental freedoms that are vital for the maintenance of a free society founded on truth. Among these issues are the rights of individuals peaceably to assemble, to enjoy freedom of speech and property, the freedom of the press, the freedom of education, and the right of the people to petition their government to redress their grievances. Only by truly and fully guaranteeing such freedoms as these can a society legitimately be a free society founded on truth. This is because social policies that restrict these freedoms through direct or indirect means, necessarily limit the pursuit of truth, resulting in a stifling of open communication, a closure of all possibilities for redress of injustices, and a loss of trust in governmental and social institutions.

Truth, on the other hand, expects and foresees that diverse people within a free society will come together frequently and sincerely to communicate with one another through a variety of avenues. A free society founded on truth preserves the right of persons to voice their opinions in respectful disagreement with one another and with their elected and appointed governing leaders. A free society founded on truth recognizes the rights of persons to enjoy the use of their home and property. A free society founded on truth recognizes that any curtailment of these civil liberties and rights substantially harms individuals specifically and the public in general. Such a curtailment is an expression of intolerance per se that denies opportunities for authentic, loving relationships among persons. Ultimately, it becomes a denial of not only the civil liberties but the truth and freedom for authentic human existence.

5. Religious Freedom as founded on truth

The reason for making a separate distinction for religious freedom as founded on truth is because of its inherently precious and sacred quality among all other civil liberties. God created us human beings fundamentally as worshipping beings. The categorization of the human being as *homo adorans*, as worshipping being, is well known. To deny this aspect of our humanity is to ultimately deny our humanity itself. Because we were also created as inherently social creatures, it follows that we were created by God to give social expression to our religious feelings through rituals, acts, and rites of worship. Though personal and certainly intimate, our worship is, at the same time, a fundamentally social, or corporate, expression of our faith. At the same time, we have been created by God as persons with free will; we have the freedom to believe in Him who created us, and we also have the freedom to reject such a belief or posit an alternative one.

Recognizing this, a society that is genuinely founded on truth preserves the freedom of persons to associate with others in the expression of their faith. Finally, a free society founded on truth must preserve the free exercise of religion without any interference from government, while at the same time it must ensure that its members also enjoy the freedom to interact within society without having religion imposed upon them against their will. Social policies and laws that deny the free exercise of religion are not acting in accordance with truth because they reject fundamental characteristics of the human person, resulting in an affront to human dignity and in an injustice of the gravest sort. Likewise, social policies and laws that subject a person to the imposition of the rules or dictates of a particular religion against his will are also devoid of truth and constitute an injustice because they diminish the ability of the person to grow in freedom and in relationship with others.

I naturally speak on the topic of religious freedom from a variety of perspectives: as a religious leader from the perspective of Orthodox Christianity, as an American citizen from the perspective of the United States Constitution, and as a native of Greece which, along with other European nations and Turkey, is a signatory to the European Convention for the Protection of Human Rights and Fundamental Freedoms, which guarantees religious freedom. Thus, I feel that I speak on the subject of religious freedom as a true citizen of the world, in both a religious and political sense. I do not feel this is unusual in any way, but rather as indicative of the universally recognized, preeminent importance of religious freedom as a foundation of truth, one that is deeply rooted, far reaching, and obligatory for discussion as we consider issues of European solidarity and enlargement. European solidarity cannot exist without a full guarantee for religious freedom.

6. Human Rights as truth

Our consideration of the fundamental aspects of truth would not be complete if we failed to include human rights. Any intelligent discussion of human rights necessarily includes areas of law and conflict resolution that have already been mentioned, such as religious freedom, property rights, and the work of reconciliation; but the topic of human rights also extends to wider concerns that implicate the good faith basis of a society's commitment to truth, freedom, and justice. Here, we may mention troubling human rights abuses such as genocide, the unjust treatment of refugees, the practice of torture or degrading treatment of those in detention, to name just a few examples.

The literature of the Old Testament and the New Testament is replete with examples that illustrate human rights issues. Examples of human rights issues in biblical literature include, for instance, the numerous stories of torture and degrading treatment of those innocent martyrs of the faith who were unjustly imprisoned or detained and the mass infanticide ordered by Herod upon receiving news of Jesus' birth in Bethlehem. The practice of crucifixion itself in Roman times can be viewed as a human rights issue. It is possible to generate an endless list of human rights abuses in biblical literature, if one takes the time. Indeed, it seems that human rights issues have been with us since the beginning of our recorded history. Where does truth stand in relation to human rights abuses and unjust practices? Truth is antithetical to these abuses and practices for a very simple reason: the truth about the dignity and absolute value of every human being prohibits any violation of human rights. A free society founded on truth that tolerates such abuses and practices, is a society that follows the way of falsehood and denial of the ultimate truth. At a minimum, a free society founded on truth will contain voices that raise awareness of the presence of abusive practices and human rights violations within its boundaries, and that call for either their abolishment or the implementation of remedial measures that bring about just satisfaction to aggrieved parties. A free society founded on truth will listen to these voices and act in accordance with them. A society that actively or passively suppresses these voices simply cannot be called free or founded on truth.

Human rights are inseparably related to the truth that is necessary for freedom because human rights speak to the most basic priorities of human life and physical security, in addition to other necessities for life such as religious freedom. Without a genuine good faith commitment to human rights, a society is simply unable to guarantee the fundamental requisites of life that are necessary, at a minimum, for authentic relationships based on love and freedom.

7. Conclusion: Truth Making People Free

It is our hope that our consideration of the above presented six existential and political aspects of truth can help us to understand more fully Jesus' statement as it applies to the larger questions of our dialogue: *And you will know the truth, and the truth will make you free* (John 8:32).

As we contemplate Jesus' statement, it is my prayer and my hope that we can all look toward a Europe that is composed of nothing less than free societies founded on the truth; societies that are acutely aware of the need for genuine dialogue, worship, reconciliation, civil liberties, religious freedom, and human rights; societies that, by the grace of God, truly make people free.

The Dynamics of the Orthodox Faith in Contemporary America

Orthodoxy in America Lecture Series

Fordham University
February 4, 2004

1. Introduction

Your Eminence, Cardinal Dulles, Your Excellency, Archbishop Migliore, Very Reverend Father Joseph McShane, President of this renowned University, Reverend Clergy, dear professors, deans, beloved students, distinguished guests, ladies, gentlemen, friends: I thank you so much for this handsome opportunity and honor to be here tonight and to deliver this lecture, the first in a promising series.

I express my sincere thanks to the Very Reverend Father Joseph McShane, S.J., the President of this University, for this invitation and for the creation of such a prestigious series of lectures under the title "Orthodoxy in America."

We have been on this campus for half an hour, having been received by the good President, and have already enjoyed the hospitality, the cordiality, and the joy of being in this place. So my thanks extend beyond the lecture hall and encompass the whole campus.

I also express my thanks to two young professors and scholars who were assigned the responsibility to organize the present lecture series, Dr. George Demakopoulos, whom I thank for the gracious introduction, and Dr. Aristotle Papanikolaou, who was one of my prominent students of theology at Holy Cross Greek Orthodox School of Theology in Brookline, Massachusetts in the late 1980s.

I feel also the honor of the presence of Cardinal Dulles, whom I remember with regard an important theological article that he wrote back in the 1960s. At that time, I could not even imagine that the author of that article would be present, forty years later, at an initial lecture on Orthodoxy as a distinguished Cardinal of the Roman Catholic Church.

This lecture falls within the annual time frame during which we celebrate the feast of the Three Hierarchs, the three great Fathers of the Church, namely, Saint Basil the Great, Saint Gregory the Theologian, and Saint John Chrysostom; in fact, it continues and concludes these celebrations. This constitutes not only a handsome coincidence, but also a blessed beginning to this new lecture series.

The title of my presentation is "The Dynamics of the Orthodox Faith in Contemporary America." This title has been purposely selected in order to indicate from the very outset that in the case of the Orthodox faith, i.e. the faith of the Orthodox Church, we do not deal with an inert, passive, ossified entity; but, rather, with something that is dynamic, full of inexhaustible energy, something involved in action and reaction, something that is an expression of vibrant life.

As such, the Orthodox faith has been fully involved in the long past, as well as in the present, in continuous life situations, challenges, provocations, persecutions of all kinds, disputes, debates, and missionary actions, in all geographical areas. It has been involved in developmental processes in new lands and countries, and in efforts to maintain its identity under any circumstances, old or new. The above mentioned challenges, actions, and life conditions in general became ways and means of the manifestations of the dynamic character of the Orthodox faith and Church, a dynamic character revealed throughout the twenty centuries of her existence, and being visible and active in contemporary America.

So then, by the title "The Dynamics of the Orthodox Faith (or Church) in Contemporary America," we mean the expression of a dynamism which produces events and conditions within the life situations and environment of contemporary America. We mean a dynamism which is in direct and uninterrupted continuity and absolute identity with the dynamism of the Orthodox faith and Church throughout the two millennia of Her life.

Obviously, there is no way for an adequate and, all the more, an exhaustive presentation of the dynamics of the Orthodox faith in contemporary America. Let me therefore be selective and, by necessity, limited, and offer to you the gracious "fellow listeners," or ὁμακόειον, to use a nice Pythagorean word repeated also by Clement of Alexandria and meaning "co-listeners" or "fellow listeners," some characteristic expressions of the dynamics of the Orthodox faith as we experience them today.

2. Expression Number One: The Dynamics of the Orthodox Faith in the Area of Language

Language is a vital expression of life. It is the main expression of communication and connectedness among human beings and between God and humanity.

Orthodoxy in the course of history has contributed immensely to the perfection of languages such as Greek, Latin, or Slavic. We think of the superb pertinent achievements in the fields of theology, poetry, and hymnography, which combine poetry and music as well. Here, we deal with thousands and thousands of pages and with myriads of ecclesiastical hymns in which the dynamics of faith helped to produce highly sophisticated linguistic achievements in terms of an amazing richness of vocabulary, a remarkably refined style, and unexpected new grammar and syntax formations. But presently, we live in America, and we have the English language. What can we say concerning the English language as a vehicle for articulating properly and beautifully the contents and verbal expressions of the Orthodox faith? And how do the dynamics of faith operate on that level?

We witness, of course, during the nineteenth and twentieth centuries the appearance of patristic works in English translations. These works have been the result of commendable academic efforts and fine scholarly publishing enterprises. The dynamics, however, of the Orthodox faith in the area of the English language manifested themselves in a constantly increasing rhythm in the twentieth century, and they continue in the present century through activities initiated, inspired, and promoted by the Church. In addition to translations from patristic works and theological books written originally in a non-English language, predominantly Greek, we have today an astonishing production of Orthodox theological books written originally in English. These books in English constitute not only significant theological works, but also excellent literary products. They cover all fields within the realm of theology; for instance, the biblical, the dogmatic, the liturgical, the pastoral, and the historical, not to mention the various combinations of theology and sociology, psychology, anthropology, environmental sciences, and even political sciences. This impressive production of Orthodox literature in the English language, be it purely theological or representing a combination of disciplines, is the result of the dynamics of the Orthodox faith. This happens predictably, one could say, in any place in which Orthodoxy is transplanted. It is an expected result.

On the other hand, one could say that we already have a very rich theological language in English, the language of hundreds of theological schools and seminaries, the language used in this University, the language of literally millions of theological books, among them true masterpieces. The observation is absolutely correct.

What, however, I am talking about is the very special nuance offered by the English language when it is employed in Orthodox theological works, be they patristic or contemporary. It is what I call the Orthodox linguistic idiom in English. This is not a linguistic peculiarity or an exotic feature. This is an enrichment I dare say, an introduction of a fresh nuance to an otherwise beautiful language, full of semantic suggestiveness and sometimes with subtle existential overtones.

Allow me at this juncture to inform you about two particular aspects related to the topic under discussion. The first is the difference between America of the 1960s and the present time in America. In the 1960s, the number of Orthodox theological books in English was small and limited mostly to translations. Today, we have a very impressive publishing activity, and we deal with voluminous catalogues of Orthodox theological and ecclesiastical works in English. Today, in the United States, we have bookstores that sell exclusively Orthodox books, and they are doing very well in terms of business. Needless to say, when we talk about Orthodox theological productions available in English, we also include by natural extension DVDs, videos, electronic media, websites, etc. Here, there is plenty of English Orthodox theological language, a result of the dynamism of the Orthodox faith.

The other relevant aspect which I should like to share with you is the translation into English of considerable amounts of Orthodox hymnological material. Here, the dynamism of the Orthodox faith in the area of language is well on its way to creating an amazing literary treasure in the English language. The amount of hymnological material is huge and highly diversified, but it is always inspiring and beautiful. Here, there is the challenge of taking truly magnificent hymns written mostly in Greek and producing English translations of them in such a way so as to be susceptible to musical manipulation and usage.

Allow me in passing to cite an example in order to show the magnitude and the difficulty of the challenge. I selected from among thousands and thousands, two verses from a hymn to the Mother of God where she is addressed with the words:

> Χρυσοπλοκότατε πύργε
> Καὶ δωδεκάτειχε πόλις.

Literally translated:

> You are a tower built and adorned with gold
> And a city with twelve protecting walls.

Please make a comparison. The original Greek even without music is full of rhythm. The English needs heavy editing to make it poetic, significant, and susceptible to musical investment.

    This challenge is truly enormous, but the attempts so far have been encouraging. We are justifiably entitled to expect in a few years, through continuous translations, revisions, and painstaking editorial work, the appearance of an amazing wealth of Orthodox hymns and hymnological texts, which will not only become an adornment to the existing corpus of Christian hymnology in the English language, but will also introduce refreshing musical creations for worship and spiritual as well as aesthetic enjoyment. This expectation is rendered feasible by the unstoppable action and inexhaustible energy of the dynamics of the Orthodox faith in the field of language.

3. **Expression Number Two: The Dynamics of the Orthodox Faith in the area of Truth**

The Orthodox Church has been from the very beginning exceedingly sensitive about the truth revealed by Christ, the Incarnate God, in the Gospel and entrusted to the Church for preservation, presentation, and dissemination. There is no need to speak elaborately on this subject or to show how the Church has made every possible effort to maintain the integrity of the revealed truth and to keep it in its fullness, undistorted, unblemished, unchanged, and absolutely precise. The tacit assumption in this case, which is also frequently explicitly formulated, is that the truth handed over to the Church by Jesus Christ the Lord is simply absolute; or, to use a hyperbolic phrase, it is absolutely, undeniably, and unequivocally absolute. As an absolute, it is unyielding to any attempt at manipulation, negotiation, or relativization.

The dynamics of the Church has functioned in this area in a superb way. From the very first steps of the new faith, there have been formidable attacks on the faith as truth, all the more as a truth that claims absoluteness and exclusivity. We could simply mention here the Gnostics among other opponents of the early Church in order to show the magnitude of anti-Church, anti-truth efforts. The Gnostics did not limit themselves to attacking directly or indirectly the fundamental dogmas and teachings of the Church; they attacked the very essence of the truth preserved by the Church. They did so by using language in such an arbitrary, inconsistent, and contradictory way that it practically destroyed any possibility to have a theologically or linguistically reasonable discussion about the content of faith as revealed truth. Let me cite here an example from a text by Basileides, the well-known Gnostic author of the second century in Alexandria, Egypt. The cited text is from the book of Hippolytos of Rome, written toward the end of the second century and the beginning of the third century. It refers to a comment offered by Basileides on the first chapter of the book of Genesis describing the creation of the world. Here is the text, and please listen to the language, language that is pushed to the extreme of negation and apophaticism.

> Since nothing existed, no matter, no substance, no non-substance, no simple, no composite, no unthinkable, no senseless, no human being, no angel, no god, noth-

> ing, nothing at all that could be named...
> the non-existing god without thinking,
> without feeling, without will, without
> choice, without suffering, without desire
> wanted to create a world...so the non-
> existing god made a non-existing world
> from non-existing entities. (Hippolytos,
> Ἔλεγχος Ζ' 20-21)

This is a specimen that is extreme, but it is an example of how to use language in such a way that destroys language. Here, there is no way to talk about the truth because language is completely destroyed as a means of conveying any truth.

We can understand, therefore, why the Church fought relentlessly against the Gnostics as well as against the other heretical groups in order to neutralize the deadly danger of totally hurting the truth of the Gospel. Already, Justin the Philosopher and Martyr, in the middle of the second century, had written against the Gnostics, followed by Irenaeos, Hippolytos, and Epiphanios. The Ecumenical Synods, starting with the first in Nicea in the year 325 A.D., are eloquent testimonies of the paramount importance ascribed to the truth of the Gospel as something absolute and inviolable. Throughout the centuries, the dynamics of the Orthodox faith kept the truth of the Gospel as a sacred, absolute tradition that was beyond any manipulation or relativization. The care and concern of the Fathers of the Church on this issue went sometimes even to minute details in order to secure the proper appearance of the written texts which dealt with matters of faith. Here is an amusing and charming example from Saint Basil the Great. Basil the Great, among the other Fathers, wrote about the essence of faith and the inviolable nature of truth, but he was so passionate about precision in language that he extended his care beyond the content of a manuscript, even to the quality of the handwriting. So, he writes the following to someone involved in the production of texts:

> Write straight and keep straightly to your lines; and let the hand neither mound of letters nor slide down hill. Do not force the pen to travel slant-wise like the crab, but proceed straight ahead as if traveling along a carpenter's rule, which everywhere preserves the even course and eliminates all irregularity. For that which is slant-wise is unbecoming, but that which is straight is a joy to those who see and read it, not permitting the eyes of those who read to bob up and down like well-sweeps. Something of the sort has happened to me when reading your writing. For since your lines rest ladderwise, when I had to pass from one to another I was obliged to lift my eyes to reach the beginning of the next line. And then when no sequence was evident at that point, I had to run back again and

seek the order, retracing my steps and "following the furrow"....Therefore write straight and do not confuse our mind by your oblique and slanting writing. (*Letter 334*, Loeb Vol. IV, 282-285)

What happens to our contemporary situation here in America concerning the issue of faith as absolute truth? The dynamics of the Orthodox faith help the Church maintain Her position regarding the truth of the Gospel as absolute, perfect, and complete. Here, the Church is aware of a very real phenomenon that is not exclusively American but international, namely, the galloping relativization of everything, including the truth. We are constantly and painfully reminded of the truly unique dialogue between Jesus Christ and Pontius Pilate, recorded in the Gospel of John: *Pilate said to Jesus, "So you are a king?" Jesus answered, "You say that I am a king. For this I was born and for this I have come into the world, to bear witness to the truth. Every one who is of the truth hears my voice." Pilate said to him: "What is truth?"* (John 18: 37-38).

Here is a truly existential confrontation: Jesus deliberately ignores the question about being king because He understands His kingship as being a heavenly and spiritual one, and declares Himself as the messenger of the heavenly truth, which is absolute. Pilate answers skeptically, if not cynically, *What is truth*?

Pilate's answer, or question, is a question that prevails in our culture today because we are aware of the degree of relativization, lying, distortion, semi-truths, quasi-truths, para-truths, truncated information, terrifying inflation, and ruthless manipulation of language. Thus, everything is relativized and conditional. Consequently, there seems to be an eclipse of the truth of the Gospel as absolute; and such an eclipse has a dramatic impact on value systems, moral principles, and theological dogmas.

The dynamics of the Orthodox faith do not allow a submission to the pressures of the relativization of truth. The story of Pontius Pilate is almost 2000 years old, yet his position did not prevail. We believe that the dynamism of the Orthodox faith will eventually and finally overcome the secular pressures to relativize divine truth. This, of course, is a matter of faith. But the Church is a Church of faith and not of yesterday, but of two thousand years.

In the final analysis, the absolute truth is not a theoretical scheme, but a living person, Christ Himself. He declared: *I am the truth* (John 14:6). And we faithfully respond with the phrase from the Epistle to the Hebrews (13:8): *Jesus Christ is the same yesterday and today and to the ages of ages.* He is the absolute, unchanging, ageless truth.

4. Expression Number Three: The Dynamics of the Orthodox Faith in the area of Spirituality

At an international conference in Northern Europe last summer organized by the Ecumenical Patriarchate, which had as its theme environmental issues related to the Baltic Sea, we had the opportunity to stop for a few hours in Helsinki, Finland. During that occasion we met for one hour with the President of Finland. We were just a small group of four bishops led by Ecumenical Patriarch Bartholomew. The President of Finland, without any delay, opened the discussion by asking: "Can you please talk about spirituality, spirituality versus the materialism and technological dominance which prevails in the contemporary world?" Thus, for one hour, in the Presidential Palace of Finland in Helsinki, we did not discuss political issues, international affairs, or social concerns, but rather Orthodox spirituality, spirituality as a *modus vivendi*, as a mental attitude, as a behavioral determinant in view of the modern conditions of life. The topic is, of course, of critical importance in today's world and in contemporary America.

The dynamism of the Orthodox faith is strongly present and active in this important issue of spirituality in our American reality. Spirituality could be defined in various ways. When we use the term "spirituality" we normally mean the practicing of prayer, of meditation, of reading religious literature, of worship, of community edification, of a sense of the sacred and the holy in the personal as well as in communal life and similar things.

Tonight, however, allow me to focus on another aspect and to approach the subject from a different avenue. Let me define spirituality as a basic Orthodox understanding of a human condition or attitude in which God is the priority. Let us then see the priority of God versus any other priority as an expression that defines and describes the dynamics of faith as spirituality.

Spirituality, as the priority of God in human life, brings to this life the sense of the holy, the beyond, the ineffable, the sacred, and the transcendent. Spirituality becomes a liberation from our bondage to material reality, and it opens refreshing perspectives beyond the palpable and statistically verifiable. The priority of God in human life as a central characteristic of spirituality is brilliantly evidenced in the lives of the martyrs and the saints. The Church offers high honor and constant homage to them because She sees them as the embodiment of the precious principle of the priority of God, the priority of God as the expression *par excellence* of spirituality in any and every human condition, even and mostly when facing death. It is important to note that the lists of saints and martyrs include people of all social strata: poor and rich alike, young and old, men and women, clergy and laity, bishops, priests, monks, theologians, soldiers, farmers, public officials, gardeners, cooks, inn-keepers, physicians, lawyers, ascetics of the desert, and people of the busy cities. We commemorate them everyday. Orthodox people live constantly in their spiritual company and feel that the dynamics of faith that has produced the hundreds of thousands of martyrs and saints in history is active also in the present time, in the present society, no matter where this society is located.

Here in America, the dynamics of Orthodoxy as spirituality, i.e. as a living witness to the priority of God in human life, following the example of the saints and martyrs, face two major challenges, among others. The first of these challenges comes from the existing and prevailing lifestyles in our society, which are characterized by a hectic rhythm of business, by the domination of technology, and by a consuming anxiety for survival and success. People seem to have no time for dealing with spiritual issues, with the meaning of their life vis-à-vis God or with what lies beyond what they see and touch. They have no time; which reminds us of the famous question posed by the French thinker Blaise Pascal: "Peut-être auront le temps de mourir?" "Perhaps, will they have time to die?" They don't have time, even to die!

Orthodoxy has no magic solution to this problem. What the Church offers is the dynamics of faith, which radically influences personal human conditions and attitudes which in turn are open to the growing of a vigorous spirituality. In this case, the dynamics of faith act as a catalyst, as a transforming factor introducing spirituality within the most technologically advanced environments and within the fully contemporary contexts of a busy life.

The second major challenge has to do with spirituality understood as a human attitude that is based upon the priority of God. The problem here is the number and attraction of priorities that claim the attention and final espousing by the people of today, especially here in America. As a result, you have plenty of wrong classifications of priorities in the lives of people; you have a loss of what is first and what comes second or third in importance; you have conflicted foci and a ruining of lives as a result of wrong priorities; you have a terrible waste of gifted individuals who have fallen victims of worthless priorities.

The dynamics of the Orthodox faith enter the scene by forcefully proposing a radical rearrangement, making God the priority. In this instance, we may very well hear the voice of Christ addressing the issue in a superb way from a different angle in the Gospel of Matthew. He says, *Do not be anxious, saying 'What shall we eat,' or 'What shall we drink,' or 'What shall we wear?'... but seek first the Kingdom of God and His righteousness, and all these things shall be yours as well* (Matthew 6: 31-33).

The Orthodox faith intensely and completely adheres to this dominical exhortation. If God and His Kingdom is the absolute priority, then any other priority of relative value will follow. Thus, spirituality, as the priority of God in life, will naturally, so to speak, create a healthy and robust inner core of properly classified values, needs, and secondary priorities of all kinds. Thus, spirituality will become not only an expression of religious devotion and experience, but also a tremendous, multifaceted enrichment of human life in all its aspects.

5. Expression Number Four: The Dynamics of the Orthodox Faith: Creating Balance and Completeness

The last expression of the dynamics of the Orthodox faith with which I should like to deal, are the dynamics creating balance and completeness or wholeness within the contents of the faith. Let me first point out that the dynamism of the Orthodox faith produces a constant energy and action that keeps the substantive contents of faith in a condition of balance and mutual control. This has been a steady phenomenon throughout the history of the Church. Orthodoxy has developed, to their maximum and optimum, all aspects of theology and Christian life: Theology in the strict sense, Christology, Pneumatology, Soteriology, Ecclesiology, Pastoral Theology, Liturgics, Patristics, Biblical Interpretation, Church History, Hagiography, Hymnology; all are parts of the contents of faith as theory and praxis. The important fact in this case is that all the above mentioned constitutive parts coexist in a balanced and homeostatic way and level. The dynamics of the Orthodox faith, for instance, did not allow an over-development of ecclesiology at the expense of Christology, nor the excessive growth of liturgics at the expense of pastoral theology. The dynamics of faith in Orthodoxy have been instrumental in maintaining a balance between monastic life and secular life, between clergy and laity under the principle of synergy, between philanthropy and social action and spiritual retreat and worshiping practices.

We can see the dynamics of balance even in specific areas like the worship or the canon law of the Church. In the realm of worship, the main liturgical forms such as Eucharistic liturgy, the service of matins, and the service of vespers present a remarkable internal balance, alternating between reading and singing, movement and immobility, biblical and hymnographic material, prose and poetry, word and silence. In the realm of canon law, one can easily detect the balance between ἀκρίβεια and οἰκονομία, which is between precise, strict application and lenient, flexible practice; between pedagogical reprimand and correctional punishment; between understanding human weakness but insisting on human perfection.

In essence, the dynamics of faith as a balancing factor reminds us of two ancient Greek admonitions, namely, "μηδὲν ἄγαν" and "πᾶν μέτρον ἄριστον," which mean, "Do not do anything in excess," and "every due measure is excellent."

The balancing effect of a dynamic faith is important in our contemporary situation in America. We have bitter experiences of excesses in the religious field and their catastrophic consequences. We are aware of the pain caused by uncontrollable behaviors or attitudes, and we know well what happens in various religious bodies when imbalances within the contexts of religious beliefs or the different experiences of religiosity become the norm and the prevailing reality. Hence the importance of a faith which presents a model of balance through its dynamics, a balance which, in a world flooded with religious excesses, becomes a truly healing commodity. The keeping of such a balance is not an easy task; but, here, is a clear manifestation of the dynamic character of faith.

Similar observations hold true for the other characteristic of the dynamics of the Orthodox faith, namely, its function as a vital agent creating completeness or wholeness. The balancing effect of the dynamic action of faith does not cut off anything from this faith. Everything is developed to completion, and everything is whole and preserves its integrity, its plentitude. Let me cite an example from the purely theological field.

As it is well known, Orthodoxy has formulated the Christological dogma in a perfect way. Both in short, creedal statements or in long, elaborate teachings, the Church has presented to the world Her belief in Christ as perfect God and perfect human being. He is the Lord. From this point of view, the Church has cultivated a Christocentric stance. This is apparent already at the end of the first century A.D., in the writings of St. Ignatius of Antioch, in which, characteristically, the name of Christ appears almost in every second line of the text. This Christocentrism, however, never became in Orthodoxy what specialists call Christomonism, which is an absolute, isolated, prevailing and exclusive worship of Jesus Christ. On the contrary, Christology has been always developed in parallel, contemporaneous ways with a perfect Trinitarian theology and a full and bright presentation of the faith in the Holy Spirit. The Church has been Christocentric, Trinity-centric, Spirit-centric. It has developed everything to perfection and completeness.

The dynamics of the Orthodox faith contributed to the preservation of the wholeness of the teaching about the Holy Trinity. It is not accidental that all the doxological exclamations in the Divine Liturgy of the Church are Trinitarian formulations, and that the central exclamation in the funeral service starts with Christ, to

Whom it is addressed, but ends with the reference to the Father and to the Holy Spirit as well. Equally important is the fact that the prayers of the Eucharistic Canon, which end with the central Christological event of the transubstantiation of the bread and wine of the Eucharist into the Body and the Blood of Christ, are addressed primarily to God the Father with the parallel mentioning of the Son and the Holy Spirit.

The wholeness, the completeness of what constitutes the essence of faith is amply demonstrated in the Orthodox faith, and is the result of its dynamic character. This wholeness, coupled with balance, is vital for contemporary Christians, especially in America, Christians who frequently suffer from inadequate forms of faith, from incomplete expressions of Christianity, which exhibit a weak Trinitarian theology, or a meager Pneumatology, or a Christomonistic predilection. The dynamics of the Orthodox faith aim at offering the complete and the whole content of divine revelation in Christ, preserved intact in its unsurpassed beauty and integrity for twenty centuries by the Church.

6. Concluding Remarks

Tonight, thanks to your kindness, I had the handsome opportunity to speak about four aspects, four expressions, four manifestations of the dynamic character of the Orthodox faith in America: a) in the area of language (the creation of an English theological Orthodox language), b) in the area of the absoluteness of the truth as revealed by God who became a human being in the person of Jesus Christ the Lord, c) in the area of spirituality understood in a special way as the priority of God, and d) in the dynamic character of faith as a balancing agent and an agent contributing to the presentation of the wholeness of faith, intact and perfect.

I did not speak, as perhaps expected, about Orthodox worship or about social issues. I did not speak about inter-Orthodox, inter-Christian, interreligious problems. I did not speak about major or minor ethical problems, or about issues of peace and war. I did not speak about the epic of the Orthodox immigrants, who came to the United States and created what they have created in the past two hundred years. I did not speak about Orthodoxy as the carrier of the amazing legacy of the Hellenistic and Greek tradition, and its tradition of language and culture. And, I did not speak about Orthodoxy as true philanthropy, as true humanism, as true understanding of what human beings, the cosmos, and God are about.

But, please remember, I just offered an introduction. And, I presuppose the long series of promising lectures that will follow and that, I am sure, will touch upon those and other very crucial and very basic aspects and will make this forum a forum of enlightenment, wisdom, and joy.

Ultimately, the presence of Orthodoxy in America could be understood in terms of a dynamic faith expressed in an all-encompassing love, a love which, according to the great Father of the Church

St. John Chrysostom, has no limit and goes beyond any measure. As he beautifully put it, "*Οὐ γὰρ ἔνι μέτρον τούτου τοῦ καλοῦ* (i.e. *ἀγάπης*). *Μέτρον ἀγάπης τό μηδαμοῦ ἵστασθαι*," "There is no measure of this good, which is love. The measure of love is not to stop anywhere" (St. John Chrysostom, *Exegesis of the Epistle to the Philippians* II, 18).

The Ecumenical Patriarchate and its Ministry of Reconciliation

Sacred Heart University
November 9, 2005

Most Reverend Bishop Lori, Esteemed President of Sacred Heart University Dr. Anthony Cernera, Distinguished Members of the Board of Trustees, Honorable Deans, Faculty and Members of the Administration, Reverend Fathers, Dear Students, Guests, Ladies and Gentlemen,

I am deeply thankful to God and to you for the honor that you as Sacred Heart University have graciously bestowed upon me today by giving me the Honorary Degree of Doctor of Humane Letters. But I am even more thankful for the opportunity simply to be with you today because it affords us all an occasion to contemplate together our common heritage as Christians. Indeed, I see this afternoon as a type of ecumenical encounter, not a formal one by any means, but, nonetheless, a significant encounter whereby we may *come and look into one another's eyes* to try to understand the complexities of our human condition, our shared Christian heritage, and the effects of two millennia of history upon it.

This warm and inviting phrase, *come and look into one another's eyes*, was used by the late Ecumenical Patriarch Athenagoras throughout his ministry in the arena of rapprochement between the Christian churches, especially between Orthodox and Roman Catholic. It is a phrase that suggests a great potential for dialogue, healing and reconciliation.

And it is fitting that we begin with this phrase because it alludes to the important and historic encounter that we should all remember between Ecumenical Patriarch Athenagoras and Pope Paul VI in 1964, an encounter that resulted in the so-termed *lifting of the anathemas* that had painfully divided the Churches of the East and West since 1054. Though in many respects life-changing, this episode between Pope Paul VI and Ecumenical Patriarch Athenagoras must not be viewed in isolation, as an encounter emerging out of happenstance. Rather, it was the result of intensive ecumenical labors for centuries by Christians of varying denominations and places in history, and which, through the power of the Holy Spirit, found expression in a visible, unifying, and palpable way. Today, I wish to talk about these and other labors which are particularly related to the multi-faceted ministry of the Ecumenical Patriarchate of Constantinople in the modern world.

The ministry of the Ecumenical Patriarchate may be aptly termed a ministry of reconciliation with three areas of focus: a) the ecumenical dialogue among Christians, b) the inter-religious dialogue among Jews, Christians, and Muslims, and c) the universal call to all human beings for reconciliation with our natural environment. I am concentrating particularly on the reconciliatory ministry of the Ecumenical Patriarchate because I have plenty of relevant data available. In several cases, I presuppose, of course, similar conciliatory involvements of the late Popes Paul VI and John Paul II.

Part A: The Ecumenical Patriarchate and the Ministry of Reconciliation

1. The Ecumenical Patriarchate and the Dialogue among Christians

As I mentioned, the history of Christian ecumenical dialogue has long-standing origins. The Ecumenical Patriarchate has been a part of the so-called "ecumenical movement" since its beginnings. Its resolute and firm commitment to ecumenical dialogue is the result of its living out its beliefs in real action. It seeks to live and breathe the prayerful petition of the Divine Liturgy of St. John Chrysostom: *For the peace of the whole world, for the stability of the holy churches of God, and for the u n i o n of all, let us pray to the Lord.* An even more expressive example is found in the Divine Liturgy of St. Basil the Great, which includes the petition, *Visit us with your goodness, Lord. Put an end to the schisms of the churches.*

The Ecumenical Patriarchate's involvement with ecumenical dialogue dates back as early as the sixteenth century with the so-called "Augsburg-Constantinople" encounter. This encounter consisted of a series of short exchanges between the Lutheran theologians of Tübingen and Ecumenical Patriarch Jeremiah II. These exchanges were of considerable interest in terms of the theological doctrinal differences and similarities posed between the Lutheran reformers and the Orthodox theologians. Though we cannot call those exchanges "dialogues" in the formal sense of the term, they were, nonetheless, cordial exchanges that were indicative of greater things to come in the history of ecumenism.

The modern ecumenical movement proper may be viewed as being formally facilitated by the 1930 Lambeth Conference of Anglican Bishops in Canterbury. Though there had been several informal exchanges in the nineteenth century between the Anglican communion and the Orthodox, the 1930 Lambeth Conference represents a significant period in the activity of the Ecumenical Patriarchate in terms of sustained ecumenical dialogue, and also as showing the role of the Ecumenical Patriarch as *primus inter pares*, or first among equals, in organizing the efforts of the other autocephalous Orthodox Patriarchates in ecumenical activity. At the 1930 Lambeth Conference, the Ecumenical Patriarch Photios II arranged for a delegation of the Orthodox Church to be sent to Canterbury under the leadership of the Patriarch of Alexandria. Here, Resolution 33 of the 1930 Lambeth Conference is particularly demonstrative. This resolution, in part, reads:

> The Conference heartily thanks the Oecumenical Patriarch for arranging in

co-operation with the other patriarchs and the autocephalous Churches for the sending of an important delegation of the Eastern Orthodox Church under the leadership of the Patriarch of Alexandria, and expresses its grateful appreciation of the help given to its Committee by the delegation, as well as its sense of the value of the advance made through the joint meetings in the relations of the Orthodox Church with the Anglican Communion (*Report of the Lambeth Conference, 1930*).

But this was certainly not the beginning of ecumenical activity with the Ecumenical Patriarchate as it concerned dialogue with other Christians. We may look to a rather prominent encyclical issued in 1920 by the Ecumenical Patriarchate addressed "Unto the Churches of Christ Everywhere," an unprecedented encyclical of global scope urging all Christian churches to take concrete actions to come closer together in their common faith. This encyclical reads, in part:

> We consider…that above all, love should be rekindled and strengthened among the churches, so that they should no more consider one another as strangers and foreigners, but as relatives, and as being a part of the household of Christ and *fellow heirs, members of the same body*

and partakers of the promise of God in Christ (Ephesians 3:6).

Since the issuance of that encyclical in 1920, followed by the 1930 Lambeth Conference, the Ecumenical Patriarchate has continued in an active role in ecumenical dialogue among Christians. Significantly, we may note its role as a founding member of the World Council of Churches in 1948, in which it is still very active, maintaining offices today at its Geneva headquarters.

In addition to these numerous inroads to dialogue that the Ecumenical Patriarchate has made with Protestant Churches, its continuing dialogue with the Roman Catholic Church since the twentieth century has resulted in a rapprochement that continues to grow with the passing of every year. The highly visible and historic meeting of Ecumenical Patriarch Athenagoras with Pope Paul VI in 1964, resulted in some very tangible expressions of dialogue and reconciliation. First, it led to the establishment of local dialogues and exchanges between theologians in various countries throughout the world. Just one year later in 1965, the North American Orthodox-Catholic Theological Consultation was established. This represents one of the longest, continuously running dialogues between Orthodox Christians and Roman Catholic Christians in the Western Hemisphere. The North American Consultation has consistently produced joint theological statements elaborating upon significant aspects of the Christian faith that have done much to nurture the bonds of unity between our two churches. Recent examples are the agreed statement of the Consultation issued in 1999, entitled "Baptism and 'Sacramental Economy,'" and the agreed statement issued in 2003, entitled *"The Filioque* – A Church Dividing Issue?" Further examples of what can be characterized as the dialogue of love between the Churches of Rome and Constantinople include, among others, two very tangible expressions. The first is the exchange of visiting delegations on the patronal feasts of the churches, the Feast of Ss. Peter and Paul on June 29, for Rome, and the Feast of St. Andrew on November 30, for Constantinople, respectively. On some occasions, these exchanges have included visits from the Pope or the Patriarch himself. A second expression of the ongoing dialogue of love between the two churches was marked by the very historic occasion of the return in November of 2004 from Rome to Constantinople of the Holy Relics of two Archbishops of Constantinople, St. Gregory the Theologian and St. John Chrysostom. This return was made possible by Pope John Paul II's gracious granting of a request made by Ecumenical Patriarch Bartholomew to return the relics of his predecessors to Constantinople after having been in Rome for over 800 years. That such a request could be made and granted is a testimony to the genuine sincerity of the dialogues between the Ecumenical Patriarchate and the Roman Catholic Church, which we pray will continue under the ministry of Pope Benedict XVI. It is also a testimony to the active presence of the

Holy Spirit in the ongoing process of the reconciliation of Christendom.

2. The Ecumenical Patriarchate and the Inter-religious Dialogue among Jews, Christians, and Muslims

In addition to the tremendous work that has been accomplished, by the grace of God, in the area of ecumenical dialogue among Christians, the Ecumenical Patriarchate's constant attention toward inter-religious dialogue is equally worthy of mention. As a citizen of Turkey, His All Holiness Ecumenical Patriarch Bartholomew has developed a natural sensitivity to the need for dialogue with Islam. This sensitivity arises not only from his many personal friendships with local people of Turkey, but also from his ideological background as a Greek Orthodox Christian living in the position of an ethnic and religious minority within a predominantly Muslim society. His commitment to dialogue with Islam is sophisticated, grounded in his Orthodox faith, and initiated with the conviction that such dialogue is necessary for the promotion of peace, justice, and tolerance in our world. It was in this spirit that Ecumenical Patriarch Bartholomew visited such Islamic countries as Bahrain (2000), Iran, Qatar, Azerbaijan, and Libya (2002-2003). Yet, his activities have gone beyond Islam and included vibrant dialogues with Judaism as well.

He organized several dialogues among Jews, Christians, and Muslims that have been of major significance in the arena of peace and tolerance. The first of these was the historic Conference on Peace and Tolerance in Constantinople in 1994, co-sponsored by the Appeal of Conscience Foundation. This Conference produced the oft-cited "Bosphorus Declaration," which affirmed the "Berne Declaration" of 1992 that "a crime committed in the name of religion is a crime against religion."

Since that meeting in 1994, Ecumenical Patriarch Bartholomew has been at the forefront of organizing international inter-religious conferences to confront the evils of religious fanaticism and intolerance. He was among the first of the major world religious personalities to organize a meeting of religious leaders from the Jewish, Christian, and Muslim faiths very soon after the tragic events of September 11, 2001. This meeting convened in Brussels, Belgium, on December 19-20, 2001, producing the "Brussels Declaration," in which it was stated: "We unanimously reject the notion that religion leads to an inevitable conflict of civilizations. To the contrary, we propagate the constructive and educational role of religion in the dialogue between civilizations."

In addition to these inter-religious gatherings, the Ecumenical Patriarchate has extended its dialogue activity to political, governmental, and economic organizations. The Ecumenical Patriarch initiated a particularly constructive dialogue nearly ten years ago with the European People's Party Christian Democrats Group of the European Parliament. Since 1996, this dialogue has grown in significance and in the numbers of its participants. Today, it may accurately be regarded as one of the European Parliament's most active, continuous, international, and inter-religious dialogues. The last meeting of this dialogue, the ninth thus far, took place in Constantinople last month. I had the honor of participating in it. The topics were "A Free Society Founded on Truth – Truth Making People Free," and "Religious Freedom – A Life-Giving European Value." I cannot begin to tell you how much this dialogue has grown in terms of the composition of its makeup on inter-religious levels, as well as by the number of highest level governmental representatives from various European nations who were in attendance as active participants. It is just another example of how dialogues, initiated by the Church, dominated by the quest for truth, and fostered by love and honesty, can become creative contributions to reconciliation and peace.

3. The Ecumenical Patriarchate and the Reconciliation of Human Beings with the Natural Environment

A third major focus of the Ecumenical Patriarchate's ministry in the modern world for global cooperation and reconciliation is the natural environment. Ecumenical Patriarch Bartholomew's commitment to the sanctity of the Creation as a gift from God that is to be protected, is reflected in his many and continuous pertinent efforts.

Starting in 1995, he began to host a series of seafaring environmental symposia, aimed at bringing together experts in religion and science, as well as political representatives, to focus attention on critical areas of environmental concern. The first symposium, for one week, took place on a boat in the Aegean Sea. Since 1995, four similar environmental symposia have followed on board vessels in the following areas of heavy environmental damage: the Black Sea (1997), the River Danube (1999), the Adriatic Sea (2002), and the Baltic Sea (2003). Additional environmental symposia are currently being planned for the Amazon River in July, 2006, and for the Caspian Sea in July, 2007, respectively.

What is significant, if not unparalleled, about these environmental symposia is the level of dialogue that takes place: There is the general dialogue between religion and science; then, the dialogue among the representatives and leaders of the monotheistic religions that are participants; the dialogue among the scientists themselves; and the dialogue among the various governmental representatives who are invited to embark upon the vessel at each port of call. Perhaps what is most significant about the level of this kind of dialogue is its universal and ultimate call to reconciliation, namely, the reconciliation between humankind and the natural environment itself. This act of reconciliation extends to all human beings in the world at all times, truly aiming toward what may best be described as an ultimate rapprochement.

Part B: The Difficult Conditions of the Ecumenical Patriarchate under which it Exercises its Ministry of Reconciliation

Perhaps the most extraordinary aspect concerning all efforts toward reconciliation and the union of all that the Ecumenical Patriarchate continuously undertakes is the fact that the Ecumenical Patriarchate has been living under very heavy and oppressive political conditions.

Sadly, and especially in the last five years, the Turkish government has intensified its efforts to restrict the free exercise of the religious activity of the Ecumenical Patriarchate. It has subjected the Ecumenical Patriarchate to even tighter regulations concerning its properties and to closer monitoring of its religious activities than perhaps ever before in its history. Let me be more specific on this issue, which deals in essence with serious deprivations of basic religious rights.

1. The Deprivation Referring to the Ecumenical Patriarchate's title "Ecumenical"

The first such deprivation is the consistent denial by the Turkish government of the Ecumenical Patriarchate's use of the title "Ecumenical." This title was granted to the Ecumenical Patriarch in the sixth century in recognition of his occupying the See of Constantinople, which was the center of the Empire, or *oikumene*. This title has been used by every other foreign government in the world to refer to the Ecumenical Patriarch, and it is universally used by the other Christian Churches to refer to the Ecumenical Patriarchate just the same. Despite this wide recognition of the Ecumenical Patriarch's status as leader of the world's 300 million Orthodox Christians, the Turkish government's official position is that the Ecumenical Patriarch is not "Ecumenical" Patriarch, but simply and only the religious leader of the Greek Orthodox minority population of Turkey, which though once numbering in the hundreds of thousands, today stands at a population of approximately 2000-3000. This policy has led to some rather embarrassing situations for the Turkish government. An example of such a situation occurred in 2003, when the Apostolic Nuncius in Ankara, Turkey, used the title "Ecumenical" to refer to the Ecumenical Patriarch in a special invitation letter. The invitation was issued for a lecture by the Ecumenical Patriarch in honor of Pope John Paul II on the occasion of the twenty-fifth anniversary of his papacy. In this instance, the Turkish government responded to the invitation by prohibiting any of its personnel from attending the event because the invitation letter used the title "Ecumenical" for Patriarch Bartholomew.

2. The Deprivation Relevant to the Ecumenical Patriarchate's Legal Status

Related to the refusal of the Turkish government to recognize the title of the Ecumenical Patriarch, but significantly more damaging, is the refusal of the Turkish government to give legal status to the Ecumenical

Patriarchate. As with all non-Muslim religious minority institutions in Turkey, the Ecumenical Patriarchate is recognized as a Turkish institution, subject to the policies and restrictions of the Turkish Office of Religious Affairs. As such, the Ecumenical Patriarchate does not enjoy a legal status as an independent entity. This affects its ability to petition the Turkish government for adequate redress. It also affects its ability to press its claims, objectively recognized as legitimate I might add, in international courts as "The Ecumenical Patriarchate." Instead, the individual person of the Ecumenical Patriarch must bear the burden of relying on his personal legal status to represent the Ecumenical Patriarchate. The Ecumenical Patriarchate, as such, does not enjoy legal personality.

3. The Restrictions on Property Ownership and Use

The third deprivation of basic religious rights is the restriction on property ownership and use. In 1936, Turkey's Law on Foundations No. 2762, placed Orthodox Christian property under the administration of a General Directorate of Foundations (Vakifs), which exists to this day. The General Directorate of Foundations has the power to dissolve foundations, seize foundation property, dismiss foundation boards of trustees without judicial decisions, and intervene in the management of foundation assets and accounts.[1] In addition, according

---

[1] 2004 E.U. Regular Report on Turkey's Progress Towards Accession, COM (2004) 656 final at 43-44.

to a 1974 ruling of Turkey's highest court, the government of Turkey forbids the buying or selling of real estate acquired by minority foundations after 1936. Property belonging to these foundations and acquired since that time has reverted to the State without remuneration.[2]

To date, a total of 136 properties belonging to one important Patriarchal entity, namely, the Baloukli hospital, have been ceded by force to the state in accordance with this ruling. The Baloukli hospital is a private hospital of the Ecumenical Patriarchate that administers care without discrimination to all Turkish citizens, with a quite advanced center for the treatment of alcoholism and drug abuse. To make matters worse, the government recently imposed an unbearable retroactive tax upon the very same Baloukli hospital, leading it to unavoidable bankruptcy.

Recently, the highest court of Turkey ruled that the government could confiscate a very large and historic orphanage belonging to the Greek Orthodox community on the island of Pringhipo on the grounds that it had fallen into disuse. In reality, the government had repeatedly refused over the course of decades to issue the necessary permits for the maintenance and repair of the structure.

Needless to say, that in addition to the Baloukli and the Pringhipo confiscations, hundreds of other

---

[2] 2000 European Commission against Racism and Intolerance, Second Report, note 15 para. 26.

Patriarchal properties have been arbitrarily confiscated in the recent years by the Turkish government.

4. The Deprivation of the Right to Education and Training of Clergy

I am concluding with one more deprivation of fundamental religious rights. This is the continuing closure of the Patriarchal Theological School of Halki, the sole seminary for the training of the Greek Orthodox clergy of the Ecumenical Patriarchate. This closure was the result of a law passed in 1971 by Turkey, and it represents more than an interference by the State in matters of education. It constitutes a direct violation of the basic right of a religious community to prepare its clergy and its spiritual leaders.

At present, there are some promising inroads that are being made toward reopening the School, but there have also been unkept promises by the government and shifting political interests that have prevented this from occurring.

Concluding Remarks

In spite of overwhelming difficulties and burdens from internal governmental conflicts, the Ecumenical Patriarchate stands today as a witness of Christian martyrdom and hope. Its achievements, efforts, and genuine desire to reconcile all human beings with one another in a spirit of love, even though it operates from a position of what the world may consider weakness, is an iconic reflection of the power of the Holy Spirit. Its agonies and joys capture what St. Paul was trying to express as he was reflecting upon the Lord's encouraging example, *My grace is sufficient for you: for my power is made perfect in weakness* (2 Corinthians 12:9). The Ecumenical Patriarchate is a modern, eloquent example of power made perfect in weakness.

For us also, the Ecumenical Patriarchate is an example of the reconciliation and love to which we are commonly called as Christians, who through coming together and looking in each other's eyes might find a common resolve to work toward the unity that has been the fervent prayer of the Lord Jesus Christ when He asked His Father that *those who believe in Him…may all be one* (John 17:20-21).

I thank you for your kind attention this afternoon, and I express to you once again my gratitude for this great academic honor that you have bestowed upon me.

Some Suggestions for Cultivating Interreligious Dialogue

Fairfield University
November 14, 2007

Esteemed President of Fairfield University, Rev. Fr. Jeffrey von Arx, S.J.; Distinguished Members of the Board of Trustees; Honorable Deans, Faculty and Members of the Administration; Reverend Clergy; Dear Students, Guests, Ladies and Gentlemen,

Allow me to express my deep thanks to you this afternoon for bestowing upon my humble person this honorary doctoral degree from the well-known Jesuit Fairfield University. I am thankful for this great honor indeed. But truthfully, I am thankful that God has granted us yet another day on this beautiful Earth, a day in which we are in the presence of one another. So, in a very real sense, I consider the occasion of this day not merely as an occasion to celebrate the achievements of any one person, but rather, as a manifestation of the very genuine and remarkable progress of our drawing closer and closer together as Christians of East and West, united by the love of Jesus Christ.

This work of coming together is a very real and occurring phenomenon, and it is only natural that it should be the subject of reflection whenever we gather together, regardless of the occasion. In my own life experience over the course of my ministry, as a layperson, as a priest, and as a bishop of the Church, I have come to realize the growing importance of dialogue between the faithful of various Christian Churches and between adherents of varying religions, namely Judaism, Christianity, and Islam. This realization has come also with the recognition that people in our contemporary world are thirsting for a genuine reconciliation and healing of so many injuries that have been brought about over the course of history, largely on account of people misunderstanding one another's differences, especially differences in religious orientation.

It is this subject of interfaith dialogue, a term which I use broadly to encompass inter-Christian dialogue as well as interreligious dialogue, which I wish to discuss this afternoon. Specifically, I should like to offer some suggestions for developing interfaith dialogue in a variety of contexts and venues. There is, of course, a difference between inter-Christian dialogue and the interreligious dialogue. However, my suggestions apply to both. It is my hope that as I offer these suggestions, we will be able to engage in the very act about which I am talking, that is, to come to a closer understanding of one another for who we truly are, and for what are our faith adherences.

**Suggestion One:
The Need to Unlearn in order to Learn**

A basic purpose of any interfaith dialogue is to know the others and their faith and religious ideas as practices. Very frequently, people participate in interfaith dialogues with strong preconceived ideas that they know well the people of other religions and their beliefs. Such an approach does not seem to be productive. In an interfaith dialogue, we need to unlearn what we supposedly know in order to know truly the fellow participants and their religious ideas and beliefs.

Here we may apply, *mutatis mutandis*, what St. Basil the Great offered as a nice advice to a young man seeking to acquire greater knowledge of God, "If you wish to learn, you must first unlearn." (*Letter to Gregorios*, Letter II, Loeb Vol. I p. 10) This very insightful phrase remains applicable for each of us today, regardless of our age, and is applicable to any interfaith dialogue. The phrase recognizes that we have been molded and fashioned by powerful influences upon our minds, particularly in the formative years of our lives. It also recognizes that without proper concern or awareness, these influences may have resulted in our deeply embedded predispositions against real, authentic learning, especially learning about people and their authentic faith.

Let us consider for a moment two telling examples: 1) A young child who grows up in a neighborhood filled with hostile conflict over land disputes between people of different ethnicities and faiths may emerge in adulthood as being predisposed toward either embracing religious fanaticism or against espousing religion altogether. The operative word here is "may." 2) A young child who grows up in a home with abusive parents or within the foster care system of a government agency, may emerge in adulthood as being predisposed toward either shunning the prospects of child-rearing or against the institution of marriage altogether. Once again, the operative word is "may." At the same time, in either of these cases, the very same formative influences may result, in the case of the first example, in a young man or woman growing up with particularly heightened sensitivities toward interfaith dialogue as a means of conflict resolution. The young man or woman in the second example may grow up to be even more dedicated a spouse and parent than perhaps otherwise.

In both examples, a high degree of "unlearning" is required before a genuine learning can even commence. In the quest to draw closer to one another, our willingness to unlearn should point us to the conclusion that even though we have all been molded by powerful influences upon our minds in our youth and throughout our adult years, there is a refreshing possibility for a new constructive approach.

By way of digression, allow me to add, that St. Basil, beyond his idea of the need to unlearn in order to learn, offers some practical advice about how to participate in any dialogue:

> And, first of all, one should take heed not to be boorish in conversation, but to ask questions without contentiousness, and answer without self-display; neither interrupting the speaker when he is saying something useful, nor being eager to

interject his own words for the sake of ostentation, but observing moderation both in speaking and in listening. One should not be ashamed to learn, nor should he grudge to teach; and if one has learned something from another, one should not conceal the fact...but one should candidly acknowledge the father of his idea. The middle tone of voice is to be preferred, neither so soft as to elude the ears, nor so loud and strong as to be vulgar. One should first reflect upon what one is going to say, and then deliver one's speech. One should be affable in conversation and agreeable in social intercourse, not resorting to wit as a means of gaining popularity, but depending upon the charm which comes from gracious politeness. On all occasions, abjure asperity, even when it is necessary to offer a rebuke; for if you first abase yourself and show humility, you will easily find your way to the heart of him who needs your ministrations. (*Letter to Gregorios*, Letter II, Loeb Vol. I, p. 18)

Our application of this sound advice is of the utmost importance in the arena of interfaith dialogue, which must begin with the presupposition that all parties to the dialogue are willing to first unlearn what they have learned. This implies honesty, consideration, frankness, a prayerful disposition, and even the willingness to accept truths which may in fact feel hurtful when they are offered in a genuine spirit of love with the aim of understanding and rapprochement. This now leads to a second suggestion which I offer as a way for further development of interfaith dialogue.

Suggestion Two:
Remember that Gaining in Knowledge in an Interfaith Dialogue Might Be Painful

This suggestion is based on a beautiful saying from the Book of Ecclesiastes. In the first chapter of that book we read: *In the abundance of wisdom is abundance of knowledge; and he that increases knowledge will increase pain:* Ὁ προστιθεὶς γνῶσιν προσθήσει ἄλγημα (1:18). It may seem paradoxical to suggest that gaining knowledge through an interfaith dialogue may entail pain. However, if we take the words of Ecclesiastes seriously, they simply state that if we desire to sincerely and genuinely go about the arduous task of knowing the others and their religious world, we must be willing to brace ourselves for a painful process. In acknowledging the need for reconciliation via dialogue, there follows the implication that at some point in history there has been a breach in a relationship which must be restored. This involves the uncovering of many painful truths. It also requires that we engage in truly honest inquiry into painful historical circumstances that are understood differently by different people for different reasons. The results of such an honest examination can add significant knowledge; but we should be ready, indeed we must be ready, to accept that our growing in knowledge will entail experiencing levels of pain. But the pain will not be debilitating. The real work of healing in interfaith dialogue is not to be found in the pleasantries of the nice hotels and dinners that might accompany interfaith gatherings. The real, substantive work of healing takes place when the issues that divide and separate us are squarely acknowledged for what they are and from where they derive. Healing comes about through a dialogue comprising patience, honest discussion, genuine love, and acceptance of discomfort and pain of such a formidable task. If we are willing, and there is no doubt about that, to engage in any genuine and productive interfaith dialogue, we must be open to painful experiences. And we should not be afraid of it.

Suggestion Three:
Prepare for Interfaith Dialogue by Honestly Trying to Understand the Religion of the Other

At first look, this may seem to be an obvious principle, and it appears like a variation of the first suggestion about the need to unlearn in order to learn. However, this is more than a variation. Examples of interfaith dialogue in history show that the very purpose of encounters between people of different religions frequently was to disprove the validity of the other faith, with the view toward convincing the other party of the superiority of the religious faith across the table. In such an adversarial context, how could constructive encounters ever begin to move toward anything resembling a genuine rapprochement, and even more toward anything resembling a genuine reconciliation?

Thanks be to God that we seem to have moved beyond such limited understandings of what it means to be in dialogue honestly. But to what extent have we truly progressed over the ages? This is an important question that remains to be examined. Today, however, I will limit my understanding of the answer to this question by focusing upon one well-established principle of interfaith dialogue. This is the principle of always entering into dialogue with the attitude of active listening, of focusing on learning about the other religion for the substantive values and messages which it brings to the table. Seek first to understand, then to be understood.

Suggestion Four:
In the Interfaith Dialogue, Always Think of the Sacredness and the Power of Human Language

In the twelfth chapter of the Gospel of Matthew, Jesus Christ offered a statement of a tremendous importance. He said, *I tell you, on the Day of Judgment people will render account of every careless word they utter; for by your words you will be justified and by your words you will be condemned."* Λέγω δὲ ὑμῖν ὅτι πᾶν ῥῆμα ἀργὸν ὃ λαλήσουσιν οἱ ἄνθρωποι ἀποδώσουσιν περὶ αὐτοῦ λόγον ἐν ἡμέρᾳ κρίσεως·

ἐκ γὰρ τῶν λόγων σου δικαιωθήσῃ, καὶ ἐκ τῶν λόγων σου καταδικασθήσῃ (Matthew 12:36-37). Language becomes the ultimate criterion in the Day of Judgment, and the responsibility for any careless or idle talk is enormous and has very grave consequences. Words are not cheap, and language is not an exercise of beating the air with non-substance.

In the Orthodox Church, we take very seriously the above-cited words of Christ about language. The amazing work of the Ecumenical Synods, searching unceasingly for the proper language in matters of faith and for the proper interpretation of the Bible, constitutes a terrific witness to the above-mentioned truth. Interfaith dialogue should involve a deep understanding of the sacredness and power of language. It should not be taken lightly.

On this occasion, we should remember that language has been central in the creation of the universe. In the first chapter of the book of Genesis, in the narrative presenting the successive stages of the creation of the world, the prevailing phase is *"and God said."* And God said, *"Let there be light."* And God said, *"Let there be a firmament."* And God said, *"Let the water bring forth swarms of living creatures."* And God said, *"Let the earth bring forth living creatures...."* *By the word of the Lord the heavens were made,* as Psalm 33:6 states. By our human word, in imitation of the word of God, especially by our language in dialogue, we can create a spiritually vital condition; we can establish an understanding of each other as persons and as religions, and build the bridges and avenues for a rapprochement and for a reconciliation.

**Suggestion Five:
Our Interfaith Dialogue Must Always be Focused on Truth**

The central component to our interfaith dialogue is a commitment to truth. Indeed, in an honest dialogue between Christians of East and West, and in an interfaith dialogue in general, it is this paramount principle that must exist as the foundation upon which we build. This is a central feature, to mention an important example, of the ongoing dialogue between Ecumenical Patriarch Bartholomew and Pope Benedict XVI, as seen in their continuing interactions with each other. Each and every time they have met, and they have met together personally on several occasions, their discussions always presuppose an uncompromising adherence to the truth.

We must, however, be careful with this issue. Truth is a concept that requires careful deliberation. Pontius Pilate asked the very same question when prompted by Christ shortly before His crucifixion. *What is truth?* But was this really a genuine question posed by Pilate in an honest search for truth? Or was it a statement rooted in cynicism, the expression of a man who for years and years was thrust into the role of settling disputes in fact and in law, weighing evidence and testimony proffered by many sides, all the while knowing full well that many decisions he reached would have political consequences? Here, "What is truth?" can clearly be understood as a cynical expression, rather than a genuine question.

Pontius Pilate's approach to truth is not and cannot be our way in dialogue with one another. For us as Christians, truth is not a murky concept, lost in a labyrinth of interpretations, trivialized or relativized. Truth is not something to be feared. We do not avoid the truth because we might consider its consequences to be negative. Rather, we begin our dialogue with the understanding that truth is a concrete notion, fulfilled in the very person of Jesus Christ the Lord. We enter into dialogue knowing that the consequences of searching for the truth will ultimately be liberating as Christ Himself said, *If you continue in my word, you are truly my disciples; and you will know the truth, and the truth will set you free* (John 8:31-32).

Interfaith dialogue, and specifically the dialogue among Christians of East and West is empty without truth. Where then is our commitment to truth to be found? How is it to be tested, cultivated and flourished? Our commitment to truth is to be found in the manner by which we explore historical events and episodes of the past, and more importantly in the manner by which we experience the love of God in our common endeavors, Whom we *worship in spirit and in truth* (John 4:24). We can say, unlike Pilate, that truth is a quality that not only is concrete and verifiable, but also liberates the soul. It is at once the object of our dialogue, and ultimately the very One whom we worship as Christians, the Lord Jesus Christ. With a firm commitment to truth, we may look upon our dialogue from an enhanced vista which is promising, refreshing, and authentically liberating.

Conclusion

These are but a few suggestions that I have shared with you this evening as ways in which we may enhance our interfaith dialogue. Each of these suggestions: a) being willing to unlearn in order to learn, b) bracing ourselves for some levels of pain, c) seeking first to understand, d) recognizing the sanctity and power of language, and e) focusing on truth; is offered in the hope that we may all continue to grow in our understanding of one another, and as Christians work for the realization of the Lord's will that *we may all be one* (John 17:21); and at the same time enhance our relationship with the non-Christians, no matter what their religion is.

And so, I close my remarks this evening with the plea for continuance: Let us continue our dialogue with one another. Let us continue to walk down a path of truth that will liberate us, unify us, and lead us to God's Kingdom, always remembering the beautiful words from Zerubbabel, the Old Testament leader, reported in the Deuterocanonical Book of First Esdras chapter 4: *But truth is great and stronger than all things. The whole earth calls upon truth and heaven blesses her. All God's works quake and tremble, and with him there is nothing unrighteous…but truth endures and is strong forever, and lives and prevails for ever and ever. With her there is no partiality or preference but she does what is righteous instead of anything that is un-*

righteous or wicked. All people approve her deeds, and there is nothing unrighteous in her judgment. To her belongs the strength and the kingship and the power and the majesty of all the ages. Blessed be the God of truth. Zerubbabel ceased speaking; *Then all the people shouted and said "Great is truth and stronger of all* (I Esdras 4:35-41).

Thank you once again for the honor bestowed on me by this dynamic Fairfield University and the joy of being with you today.

Τά Ἀνθρώπινα Ἀδιέξοδα καί οἱ Πατέρες τῆς Ἐκκλησίας

Πανεπιστήμιον Κύπρου
26 Ιανουαρίου 2006

Εἰσαγωγικά

Τά πάσης φύσεως ἀδιέξοδα ἀπετέλεσαν, ἀποτελοῦν καί θά ἐξακολουθήσουν νά ἀποτελοῦν, ὅσο ὑπάρχει ὁ κόσμος, ἀναπόσπαστο στοιχεῖο τῆς ἀνθρώπινης ζωῆς. Στοιχεῖο ὀδυνηρώτατο μέν, ἀλλά ἀναπόφευκτο.

Τό ἀναπόφευκτο τῶν ἀδιεξόδων ὀφείλεται κατά βάθος στήν ἀνθρώπινη ὑπόσταση καί κατάσταση. Ὑπαρξιακοί φιλόσοφοι τοῦ 20οῦ αἰῶνος ὅπως οἱ Martin Heidegger, Karl Jaspers καί Jean Paul Sartre, καί πρίν ἀπ' αὐτούς ὁ Sören Kierkegaard, ὡμίλησαν ἐκτενῶς καί ἀναλυτικά γιά τίς λεγόμενες ὁριακές ἀνθρώπινες καταστάσεις ὅπως εἶναι ὁ πόνος, ἡ ἀγωνία, ἡ ἐνοχή καί ὁ θάνατος. Οἱ καταστάσεις αὐτές εἶναι γιά τούς ὑπαρξιακούς φιλοσόφους μή ὑπερνικήσιμες γι' αὐτό καί τίς ὠνόμασαν ὁριακές. Ὁ ἄνθρωπος, λόγῳ ἀκριβῶς αὐτῶν τῶν ἀνυπέρβλητων καταστάσεων πού ἀντιμετωπίζει ὡς ἄτομο καί ὡς κοινωνικό ὄν, δηλαδή τοῦ πόνου, τῆς ἀγωνίας, τῆς ἐνοχῆς καί τοῦ θανάτου εὑρίσκεται αὐτομάτως καί ἀναποφεύκτως ἐνώπιον πάσης μορφῆς καί οὐσίας ἀδιεξόδων.

Πολύ πρίν από τούς υπαρξιακούς φιλοσόφους, οι Πατέρες της Εκκλησίας είχαν περιγράψει κατ' ουσίαν καί μέ τρόπο απαράμιλλο, αλλά χρησιμοποιώντας διαφορετική γλώσσα καί ορολογία, τίς ανθρώπινες υπαρξιακές καταστάσεις πού δημιουργούν αδιέξοδα. Ωμίλησαν γιά τήν ευπερίστατον αμαρτίαν (Εβρ. 12,1), γιά τό εγκόσμιο κακό καί γιά τήν τραγωδία της θνητότητος του ανθρώπου. Γιά τούς Πατέρας της Εκκλησίας τά τρία αυτά, αμαρτία, κακό, θνητότης συνυπάρχοντα καί συνδυαζόμενα προκαλούν μέ τρόπο αδυσώπητο καί σχεδόν νομοτελειακό τίς απίθανες σειρές ανθρωπίνων αδιεξόδων. Αδιεξόδων τά οποία αναφέρονται σέ προσωπικά, κοινωνικά ή καί εθνικά θέματα, καί επηρεάζουν άμεσα καί δραστικά τήν ζωή ατόμων καί συνόλων.

Οι Πατέρες της Εκκλησίας ωμίλησαν καί έγραψαν, εκτενώς καί εις βάθος, γιά τά ανθρώπινα αδιέξοδα εκφράζοντας μέ τρόπο συγκλονιστικό τήν οδύνη τους γιά τήν δοκιμασία καί θλίψη τών ανθρώπων ενώπιον αδιεξόδων ή καί δυσεπίλυτων προβλημάτων. Παράλληλα όμως οι μεγάλοι Πατέρες έγραψαν καί ωμίλησαν μέ πάθος καί πειστικότητα γιά τήν δυνατότητα καί τούς τρόπους υπερβάσεως τών ανθρωπίνων αδιεξόδων καί υπερνικήσεως τών προβλημάτων πού απορρέουν εξ αυτών.

Επιτρέψατέ μου νά παρουσιάσω μέ άκρα συντομία μερικά συγκεκριμένα Πατερικά παραδείγματα διαφόρων τύπων ανθρωπίνων αδιεξόδων καί συναφούς υπερβάσεώς των. Θά περιορισθώ μόνο σέ αναφορές πού προέρχονται από κείμενα τριών μεγάλων Πατερικών μορφῶν, ἤτοι τοῦ Ἁγίου Ἰωάννου Χρυσοστόμου, τοῦ Μεγάλου Βασιλείου καί τοῦ Ἁγίου Γρηγορίου τοῦ Θεολόγου. Οἱ Τρεῖς αὐτοί μέγιστοι φωστῆρες καί οἰκουμενικοί Διδάσκαλοι μᾶς προσφέρουν πλουσιώτατο ὑλικό σχετικό μέ τό θέμα μας. Ἄλλωστε ἡ ἐγγίζουσα ἑορτή των, ἑορτή τῶν Τριῶν Ἱεραρχῶν καί τῶν Γραμμάτων τούς εἰσάγει στήν ἄμεση ἐπικαιρότητα. Περιττόν νά λεχθῇ ὅτι τά πατερικά παραδείγματα πού θά μνημονευθοῦν στήν συνέχεια τῆς παρούσης ὁμιλίας ἔχουν ἐπιλεγῆ ἀπό ἕνα τεράστιο σέ πλοῦτο καί ποικιλία ὑλικό καί γι' αὐτό εἶναι σαφῶς περιορισμένης ἐκτάσεως. Ἁπλῶς ἀποτελοῦν χαρακτηριστικά δείγματα.

Ὁ Ἅγιος Ἰωάννης ὁ Χρυσόστομος καί τά ἀνθρώπινα ἀδιέξοδα

Γιά τόν Χρυσόστομο ἕνα κεντρικό καί μόνιμο στοιχεῖο ἀδιεξόδου εἶναι ἡ ἀπελπιστικά χαμηλή ἠθική κατάσταση τοῦ ἀνθρώπου. Στήν 4η ἑρμηνευτική ὁμιλία του στό κατά Ματθαῖον Εὐαγγέλιον, ὁ ἱερός Πατήρ ἀπευθυνόμενος στόν ἄνθρωπο τῆς πτώσεως καί ἁμαρτίας χρησιμοποιεῖ ἐντονώτατη γλῶσσα γιά νά περιγράψῃ τό ἀβυσσαλέο βάθος τῆς ἠθικῆς κατωτερότητος καί διαφθορᾶς. Στόν ἄνθρωπο αὐτό ὁ Χρυσόστομος μέ βαθύτατο πόνο λέγει·

Οὐδέ γάρ εἰ ἄνθρωπος εἶ, σαφῶς δύναμαι μαθεῖν. Ὅταν γάρ λακτίζῃς μέν ὥσπερ ὄνος, σκιρτᾷς δέ ὥσπερ ταῦρος

... γαστριμαργῆς μέν ὥσπερ ἄρκτος, πιαίνης δέ τήν σάρκα ὥσπερ ἡμίονος· μνησικακῆς δέ ὥσπερ κάμηλος· καί ἁρπάζης μέν ὡς λύκος, ὀργίζῃ δέ ὡς ὄφις, πλήττης δέ ὡς σκορπίος, ὕπουλος δέ ἧς ὥσπερ ἀλώπηξ, ἰόν δέ πονηρίας διατηρῆς ὥσπερ ἀσπίς καί ἔχιδνα, πολεμῆς δέ κατά τῶν ἀδελφῶν ὥσπερ ὁ πονηρός δαίμων ἐκεῖνος· πῶς δυνήσομαί σε μετά τῶν ἀνθρώπων ἀριθμεῖν, οὐκ ὁρῶν ἐν σοί τῆς τοιαύτης φύσεως τούς χαρακτῆρας; Τί γάρ σε εἴπω; Θηρίον; Ἀλλά τά θηρία ἑνί τούτων τῶν ἐλαττωμάτων κατέχεται· σύ δέ ὁμοῦ συμφορήσας πάντα, πορρωτέρω τῆς ἐκείνων ἀλογίας ὁδεύεις. Ἀλλά δαίμονά σε προσείπω; Ἀλλά δαίμων οὔτε γαστρός δουλεύει τυραννίδι, οὔτε χρημάτων ἐρᾷ. Ὅταν οὖν καί θηρίων καί δαιμόνων ἐλαττώματα πλείονα ἔχῃς, πῶς σε ἄνθρωπον καλέσομεν, εἰπέ μοι; Καί τό δή χαλεπώτερον, ὅτι οὕτω διακείμενοι κακῶς, οὐδέ ἐννοοῦμεν τῆς ψυχῆς ἡμῶν τήν ἀμορφίαν, οὐδέ καταμανθάνομεν αὐτῆς τό δυσειδές. Τῆς ψυχῆς ἡμῶν οὐκ ἀμόρφου μόνον, ἀλλά καί θηριομόρφου γεγενημένης, οὐδέ μικρόν αἰσθανόμεθα. (Ὁμιλία 4 εἰς τό κατά Ματθαῖον Εὐαγγέλιον, Migne P.G. 57, 48-49)

Ἀσχέτως τῆς ρητορικῆς ὑπερβολῆς πού χρησιμοποιεῖ ἐδῶ, ὁ Χρυσόστομος περιγράφει εὔγλωττα καταστάσεις ἀπελπιστικά χαμηλῆς ἠθικῆς καί γενικώτερα ἀνθρώπινης ποιότητος. Οἱ καταστάσεις αὐτές, ὅπως σέ κάθε βῆμα τονίζει, εἶναι γενετικές ἀδιεξόδων τόσο στό προσωπικό ὅσο καί στό κοινωνικό ἐπίπεδο προκαλώντας χρόνια ἐνδοοικογενειακά προβλήματα, ὀξύτατες συγκρούσεις μεταξύ κοινωνικῶν ὁμάδων καί αἱματηρούς πολέμους μεταξύ ἐθνῶν. Ἐκ πρώτης ὄψεως φαίνεται νά ἔχουν ἀναφορά στό ἄτομο, ἀλλά εἶναι προφανές ὅτι λόγῳ τοῦ εἴδους των ἔχουν βαρύτατες ἐπιπτώσεις στό σύνολο.

Πῶς ἀντιμετωπίζει ὁ ἱερός Πατήρ τίς παραπάνω καταστάσεις, οἱ ὁποῖες ἀναντιρρήτως ἀποτελοῦν σοβαρώτατα ὑπαρξιακά προβλήματα τά ὁποῖα συχνά μεταβάλλονται σέ ἀδιέξοδα;

Θά μπορούσαμε, ἁπλουστεύοντας καί συμπυκνώνοντας στό ἔπαρκο τίς σχετικές ἀπόψεις του νά ἐπισημάνουμε δύο κεντρικές θέσεις του, οἱ ὁποῖες μετατρέπουν τά ἀδιέξοδα σέ προβλήματα δεκτικά λύσεως καί ὑπερβάσεως. Ἡ πρώτη θέση, τήν ὁποία ὁ Χρυσόστομος ἀναπτύσσει μέ ἰδιαίτερη ἔμφαση στήν ἑρμηνεία τῆς πρός Ρωμαίους ἐπιστολῆς τοῦ Ἀποστόλου Παύλου, εἶναι ὅτι ἡ ὑπέρβαση τῶν ἀδιεξόδων μπορεῖ νά πραγματοποιηθῇ διά τῆς πίστεως στό Θεό. Ἡ πίστη γι' αὐτόν ἀποτελεῖ μοναδική δυνατότητα μεταμορφώσεως τοῦ ἀνθρώπου καί τῶν καταστάσεων ἀδιεξόδου πού ἀντιμετωπίζει. Πρέπει βεβαίως νά λεχθῇ ὅτι γιά τόν ἱερό Χρυσόστομο ἡ πίστη δέν εἶναι μιά ἁπλή θρησκευτική διάθεση οὔτε φαινόμενο ένδεικτικό παθητικότητος, νωθρότητος, φυγής, άδυναμίας ή διανοητικής άδράνειας. Όλως άντιθέτως, ή πίστη είναι έκφραση δυνάμεως, σοφίας καί ευγένειας ψυχής πού άκτινοβολεϊ τήν άλήθεια ότι «τά άδύνατα δύναται Θεός» (Πρός Ρωμαίους, Ομιλία 8, Migne P.G. 60, 455).

Προκειμένου νά καταστήσει άπολύτως σαφές καί άνεπίδεκτο άμφισβητήσεως τό σημείο αύτό, ό ιερός Πατήρ όμιλεϊ διά μακρών περί τού Αβραάμ, πού δεσπόζει ώς μορφή στό τέταρτο κεφάλαιο τής πρός Ρωμαίους Επιστολής τού Αποστόλου Παύλου. Καί δείχνει πειστικά ότι ή πίστη τού Αβραάμ ένώπιον ένός τρομερού άδιεξόδου πού άντιμετώπιζε, ήταν έκφραση «γενναιοτάτης ψυχής καί φιλοσόφου γνώμης καί ύψηλής διανοίας. Τό μέν γάρ μή κλέψαι μηδέ φονεύσαι, καί τών τυχόντων έστί· τό δέ πιστεύσαι, ότι τά άδύνατα δύναται Θεός, μεγαλοφυούς τινος δείται ψυχής, καί σφόδρα περί αύτόν διακειμένης» (Πρός Ρωμαίους, Ομιλία 8, Migne P.G. 60, 455)

Στό σημείο αύτό ό Χρυσόστομος θά διατυπώσει μέ παρρησία τήν βεβαιότητά του γιά τήν ευγένεια καί μεγαλοφυΐα τής πίστεως καί γιά τήν άπόλυτη δύναμή της νά όδηγήσῃ τόν άνθρωπο άπό τό άδιέξοδο στό άνοιγμα έξόδου σωτηρίας.

Βεβαίως ή διά τής πίστεως ριζική άλλαγή τών άνθρωπίνων συνθηκών είναι έν τελική άναλύσει έργο τού Θεού έν Χριστώ Ίησού. Γράφει σχετικά ό Χρυσόστομος:

Κἄν Ἕλλην (δηλ. εἰδωλολάτρης) ἦς, κἄν πᾶσαν ἐπελθών κακίαν, κἄν Σκύθης, κἄν βάρβαρος, κἄν αὐτοθηρίον, κἄν πάσης ἀλογίας γέμων, καί μυρία ἁμαρτημάτων ἐπιφερόμενος φορτία, ἅμα τόν περί σταυροῦ λόγον κατεδέξω καί ἐβαπτίσθης, καί πάντα ἐκεῖνα ἐξήλειψας . . . Δικαιοσύνη γάρ Θεοῦ ἐν αὐτῷ ἀποκαλύπτεται . . . Καί δικαιοσύνη οὐ σή, ἀλλά Θεοῦ, καί το δαψιλές αὐτῆς καί το εὔκολον αἰνιττόμενος (ὁ Παῦλος). Οὐ γάρ ἐξ ἱδρώτων καί πόνων αὐτήν κατορθοῖς, ἀλλ' ἀπό τῆς ἄνωθεν δωρεᾶς λαμβάνεις, ἕν μόνον εἰσφέρων οἴκοθεν, τό πιστεῦσαι (Πρός Ρωμαίους, Ὁμιλία 2, Migne P.G. 60, 408-9).

Ἡ δεύτερη θέση στήν ὁποία ὁ Χρυσόστομος ἐπιμένει σέ κάθε κείμενό του εἶναι ἡ δυνατότητα ὑπερβάσεως τῶν ἀδιεξόδων διά τῆς ἀποφασιστικῆς συμβολῆς τοῦ ἀνθρωπίνου παράγοντος τόν ὁποῖο ὀνομάζει *προαίρεσιν*.

Προαίρεσις γι' αὐτόν σημαίνει ἐλεύθερη ἐκλογή, ἐσκεμμένη καί σκόπιμη ἐπιλογή, ἐλευθερία ἀποφάσεως. Ἡ λέξη αὐτή ἦταν ἤδη γνωστή μέσῳ τῆς κλασικῆς παραδόσεως (π.χ. Πλάτων, Ἀριστοτέλης, βλ. Πλάτωνος, *Παρμενίδης*, 143C, Ἀριστοτέλους, *Πολιτικά* 1280α34.), καθώς ἐπίσης καί μέσῳ μερικῶν παλαιῶν ἐκκλησιαστικῶν συγγραφέων πού προηγήθηκαν τοῦ Χρυσοστόμου (ὡς π.χ. Ἰουστῖνος, Κλήμης Ἀλεξανδρεύς, Τατιανός, Ὠριγένης, Μέγας Ἀθανάσιος, Γρηγόριος Νύσσης, βλ. Ἰουστίνου Μάρτυρος, *Διάλογος πρός Τρύφωνα*, 88, 5· Κλήμεντος Ἀλεξανδρέως, *Στρωματεῖς*, 4-6· Τατιανοῦ, *Πρός Ἕλληνας*, 7· Ὠριγένους, *Περί ἀρχῶν*, 3.1.24· Μεγάλου Ἀθανασίου, *Λόγος περί τῆς ἐνανθρωπήσεως τοῦ Λόγου*, P.G. 25, 101C· Γρηγορίου Νύσσης, *Λόγος Κατηχητικός*, P.G. 45, 77A.) Στόν Χρυσόστομο, ὅμως, καί ἰδιαίτερα στήν ἑρμηνεία του τῆς *πρός Ρωμαίους Ἐπιστολῆς*, ὁ ὅρος προαίρεσις γίνεται ὅρος ὑψηλῆς συχνότητος ὁ ὁποῖος ὑπονοεῖ ἕνα συνδυασμό στοιχείων βουλητικῶν, διανοητικῶν καί συναισθηματικῶν. Γιά τόν Χρυσόστομο, προαίρεση εἶναι ὁ πυρήνας τοῦ ἀνθρώπινου ὄντος, ἡ ἀναπαλλοτρίωτη βασική ἰδιότης του καί ἡ οὐσία τῆς γνήσιας ταυτότητός του. Ἡ προαίρεση προσφέρει, ἀπό τήν ἀνθρώπινη ἄποψη, τόν ἀπαραίτητο παράγοντα γιά τήν μεταμόρφωση τόσο τοῦ ἴδιου τοῦ ἑαυτοῦ του ὅσο καί τῶν προβλημάτων καί ἀδιεξόδων του. Γιά νά τονίσῃ τήν ἀποφασιστική σημασία τῆς προαιρέσεως ὁ ἱερός Πατήρ χρησιμοποιεῖ τό παράδειγμα τοῦ πολύτιμου λίθου ἀδάμαντος. Γράφει σχετικῶς: «Οὐκ ὁρᾷς τόν ἀδάμαντα ἐν τῷ παίεσθαι πλήττοντα; Ἀλλ' ἡ φύσις φησί, τοῦτο ἔχει. Ἀλλά καί σοί δυνατόν ἐν τῇ προαιρέσει γενέσθαι τοιοῦτον, ὅπερ ἀπό φύσεως ἐκείνῳ (δηλ. τῷ ἀδαμάντι) συμβαίνει» (*Πρός Ρωμαίους, Ὁμιλία* 3, Migne PG 60, 416). Ἡ προαίρεση μπορεῖ νά ἀλλάξῃ ἀκόμη καί αὐτή τή φύση, δηλαδή τά φυσικά ἀνθρώπινα δεδομένα, ἔκφραση τῶν ὁποίων ἀποτελοῦν καί τά ἀδιέξοδα. Γιά τόν Χρυσόστομο ἡ συνεργία ἀνθρωπίνης προαιρέσεως καί θείας δυνάμεως παρέχει τήν βεβαιότητα ἀντιμετωπίσεως τῶν πάσης φύσεως ἀδιεξόδων.

Ὁ Μέγας Βασίλειος καί τά ἀνθρώπινα ἀδιέξοδα

Στήν πολυκύμαντη καί ἐκπληκτική ζωή του ὁ Μέγας Βασίλειος εὑρέθηκε ἐνώπιον πλήθους ἀδιεξόδων πού καλύπτουν ἕνα εὐρύτατο φάσμα. Ἀδιέξοδα ἀναφερόμενα σέ θέματα πίστεως, γνώσεως, ἐκκλησιαστικῆς καταστάσεως, ἀνθρώπινης συμπεριφορᾶς, σέ θέματα προσωπικά καί κοινωνικά, σέ θέματα βασανιστικῶν ἀσθενειῶν, ἀδίκων ἐξοριῶν καί πικρῶν θανάτων. Διαβάζοντας τά ἀριστουργηματικά συγράμματά του μπορεῖ κανείς νά σχηματίσῃ μιά εἰκόνα γιά τό πλῆθος τῶν προβλημάτων πού συνάντησε σέ κάθε του βῆμα, προβλημάτων τά ὁποῖα σέ πολλές περιπτώσεις συνιστοῦσαν κατ' οὐσίαν ἀδιέξοδα.

Ἐκεῖ ὅμως, ὅπου προβάλλει ἀνάγλυφα ἡ πραγματικότητα τῶν μεγάλων προβλημάτων καί ἀδιεξόδων, εἶναι οἱ ἐπιστολές τοῦ Μ. Βασιλείου. Στίς 368 σωζόμενες ἐπιστολές του ὑπάρχουν διάσπαρτα στοιχεῖα αὐτοῦ τοῦ φαινομένου. Ὁ προσωπικός χαρακτῆρας τῶν ἐπιστολῶν του τίς καθιστᾶ περισσότερο ἀποκαλυπτικές τῶν ἀδιεξόδων πού ἔπρεπε νά ὑπερνικήσῃ ὁ μεγάλος αὐτός ἀγωνιστής τῆς πίστεως, τῆς ἀληθείας καί τῆς ἀνθρώπινης ἀξιοπρεπείας.

Στό σημεῖο αὐτό θά μποροῦσαν νά ἀναφερθοῦν δύο χαρακτηριστικά παραδείγματα.

Τό πρώτο σχετίζεται μέ τό τραγικό αδιέξοδο πού δημιουργήθηκε στίς Εκκλησίες εξ αιτίας τής μανίας καί τής εκτάσεως τῶν αιρέσεων. Γράφει σχετικά στήν ὑπ' ἀριθμόν 90 Ἐπιστολή του (*Τοῖς Ἁγιωτάτοις Ἀδελφοῖς καί Ἐπισκόποις τοῖς ἐν τῇ Δύσει*):

> Κέκμηκε γάρ ἐνταῦθα, ἀδελφοί τιμιώτατοι, καί ἀπείρηκε πρός τάς συνεχεῖς προσβολάς τῶν ἐνεντίων ἡ Ἐκκλησία, ὥσπερ τι πλοῖον ἐν πελάγει μέσῳ ταῖς ἐπαλλήλοις πληγαῖς τῶν κυμάτων βασανιζόμενον, εἰ μή τις γένοιτο ταχεῖα ἐπισκοπή τῆς ἀγαθότητος τοῦ Κυρίου . . . Γνώριμα δέ τά θλίβοντα ἡμᾶς, κἄν ἡμεῖς μή λέγωμεν· εἰς πᾶσαν γάρ τήν οἰκουμένην ἐκκέχυται. Καταπεφρόνηται τά τῶν Πατέρων δόγματα, ἀποστολικαί παραδόσεις ἐξουθένηνται, νεωτέρων ἀνθρώπων ἐφευρέματα ταῖς Ἐκκλησίαις ἐμπολιτεύεται· τεχνολογοῦσι λοιπόν, οὐ θεολογοῦσιν οἱ ἄνθρωποι· ἡ τοῦ κόσμου σοφία τά πρωτεῖα φέρεται, παρωσαμένη τό καύχημα τοῦ σταυροῦ. Ποιμένες ἀπελαύνονται, ἀντεισάγονται δέ λύκοι βαρεῖς, διασπῶντες τό ποίμνιον τοῦ Χριστοῦ. Οἶκοι εὐκτήριοι ἔρημοι τῶν ἐκκλησιαζόντων, αἱ ἐρημίαι πλήρεις τῶν ὀδυρομένων. Οἱ πρεσβύτεροι ὀδύρονται, τά παλαιά

συγκρίνοντες τοῖς παροῦσιν· οἱ νέοι ἐλεινότεροι, μή εἰδότες οἵων ἐστέρηνται.

Ὁ ἱερός Πατήρ ἐπανέρχεται στό θέμα αὐτό στήν ὑπ' ἀριθμόν 92 Ἐπιστολή του (*Πρός Ἰταλούς καί Γάλλους*) ὅπου γράφει:

Οὐ γάρ περί μιᾶς Ἐκκλησίας ὁ κίνδυνος, οὐδέ δύο ἤ τρεῖς αἱ τῷ χαλεπῷ τούτῳ χειμῶνι περιπεσοῦσαι. Σχεδόν γάρ ἀπό τῶν ὅρων τοῦ Ἰλλυρικοῦ μέχρι Θηβαΐδος τό τῆς αἱρέσεως κακόν ἐπινέμεται. Ἧς τά πονηρά σπέρματα πρότερον μέν ὁ δυσώνυμος Ἄρειος κατεβάλετο· ῥιζωθέντα δέ διά βάθους ὑπό πολλῶν τῶν ἐν μέσῳ φιλοπόνως τήν ἀσέβειαν γεωργησάντων, νῦν τούς φθοροποιούς καρπούς ἐξεβλάστησαν. Ἀνατέτραπται μέν τά τῆς εὐσεβείας δόγματα, συγκέχυνται δέ Ἐκκλησίας θεσμοί ... Οἴχεται σεμνότης ἱερατική, ἐπιλελοίπασιν οἱ ποιμαίνοντες μετ' ἐπιστήμης τό ποίμνιον τοῦ Κυρίου, οἰκονομίας πτωχῶν εἰς ἰδίας ἀπολαύσεις καί δώρων διανομάς παραναλισκόντων ἐπί τῶν φιλαρχούντων. Ἡμαύρωται κανόνων ἀκρίβεια, ἐξουσία τοῦ ἁμαρτάνειν πολλή ... Ἀπόλωλε κρῖμα δίκαιον, πᾶς τις τῷ θελήματι της καρδίας αύτοῦ πορεύεται. Ἡ πονηρία ἄμετρος, οἱ λαοί ἀνουθέτητοι, οἱ προεστῶτες ἀπαρρησίαστοι. Διό καί ἄσπονδός ἐστιν ὁ πόλεμος οὗτος, τῶν τά πονηρά εἰργασμένων τήν κοινήν εἰρήνην ὡς ἀποκαλύπτουσαν αὐτῶν τά κρυπτά τῆς αἰσχύνης ὑφορωμένων. Ἐπί τούτοις γελῶσιν οἱ ἄπιστοι, σαλεύονται οἱ ὀλιγόπιστοι· ἀμφίβολος ἡ πίστις, ἄγνοια κατακέχυται τῶν ψυχῶν. . . . . Σιγᾷ μέν γάρ τῶν εὐσεβούντων στόματα, ἀνεῖται δέ πᾶσα βλάσφημος γλῶσσα· ἐβεβηλώθη τά ἅγια, φεύγουσι τούς εὐκτηρίους οἴκους οἱ ὑγιαίνοντες τῶν λαῶν ὡς ἀσεβείας διδασκαλεῖα, κατά δέ τάς ἐρημίας πρός τόν ἐν τοῖς οὐρανοῖς Δεσπότην μετά στεναγμῶν καί δακρύων τάς χεῖρας αἴρουσιν.

Καί προσθέτει στήν ὑπ' ἀριθμόν 243 Ἐπιστολή του (*Πρός Ἰταλούς καί Γάλλους Ἐπισκόπους περί τῆς καταστάσεως καί συγχύσεως τῶν Ἐκκλησιῶν*):

Διωγμός κατείληφεν ἡμᾶς, ἀδελφοί τιμιώτατοι (λόγῳ τῶν αἱρέσεων) καί διωγμῶν ὁ βαρύτατος. Διώκονται γάρ ποιμένες, ἵνα διασκορπισθῶσι τά ποίμνια . . . . Ἦχος θρηνούντων ἐν πόλει, ἦχος ἐν ἀγροῖς, ἐν ὁδοῖς, ἐν ἐρημίαις. Μία φωνή ἐλεεινή πάντων τά σκυθρωπά φθεγγομένων. Ἐξῆρται χαρά καί εὐφροσύνη πνευματική. Εἰς πένθος ἐστράφησαν ἡμῶν αἱ ἑορταί, οἶκοι προσευχῶν ἀπεκλείσθησαν, ἀργά τά θυσιαστήρια τῆς πνευματικῆς λατρείας. Οὐκέτι σύλλογοι χριστιανῶν, οὐκέτι διδασκάλων προεδρίαι, οὐ διδάγματα σωτήρια, οὐ πανηγύρεις, οὐκ ὑμνῳδίαι νυκτεριναί, οὐ τό μακάριον ἐκεῖνο τῶν ψυχῶν ἀγαλλίαμα ὅ ἐπί τοῖς συνάξεσι καί τῇ κοινωνίᾳ τῶν πνευματικῶν χαρισμάτων ταῖς ψυχαῖς ἐγγίνεται τῶν πιστευόντων εἰς Κύριον. Ἡμῖν πρέπει λέγειν ὅτι· «Οὐκ ἔστιν ἐν τῷ καιρῷ τούτῳ ἄρχων οὔτε προφήτης οὔτε ἡγούμενος οὔτε προσφορά οὔτε θυμίαμα, οὐ τόπος τοῦ καρπῶσαι ἐνώπιον Κυρίου καί εὑρεῖν ἔλεος» (Δανιήλ, 3, 38 - Προσευχή Ἀζαρίου 1,15).

Ἐν ὄψει τῶν φοβερῶν αὐτῶν καταστάσεων ἀδιεξόδων ὁ Μ. Βασίλειος τονίζει μέ ὅλη του τήν δύναμη ὅτι γιά τήν ὑπερνίκησή των ὑπάρχει ἐπείγουσα ἀνάγκη ἐντάσεως τῆς πίστεως στόν Θεό, αὐξήσεως τῆς ἰσχύος τῆς καρτερίας καί ἐλπίδος, ἐπιμονῆς στήν προσευχή καί ἀγῶνος διά τοῦ λόγου τῆς ἀληθείας, τήν ὁποία κατέχει ἡ Ἐκκλησία. Ἐκεῖ ὅπου σπείρεται τό ψεῦδος καί ἡ πλάνη σπείρατε τήν ἀλήθεια πού ἐλευθερώνει, φωνάζει ὁ Μ. Βασίλειος.

Έκεῖ ὅπου τό στόμα τῶν ἀσεβῶν «λαλεῖ μάταια» καί ἀνοίγει ἀνίατες πληγές λαλήσετε δικαιοσύνην καί ἀγάπην Θεοῦ.

Ὁ ἱερός Πατήρ μέ τίς ἐπιστολές του πρός ὅλες τίς Ἐκκλησίες καλεῖ σέ ἐπαγρύπνηση καί συνεχῆ μάχη. Γράφει χωρίς ἀνάπαυση, προσφέροντας ἰσχυρά ἐπιχειρήματα στούς ἀγωνιζόμενους γιά τήν ὑπερνίκηση τῶν ἀδιεξόδων πού ἡ αἵρεση καί ἡ πλάνη δημιούργησαν.

Τό δεύτερο παράδειγμα ἀπό τόν Μ. Βασίλειο στό ὁποῖο ἀξίζει νά γίνη μιά σύντομη ἀναφορά, σχετίζεται μέ ἕνα ἄλλου εἴδους ἀδιέξοδο, τό ὁποῖο ἔχει προσωπικό χαρακτῆρα. Στήν ὑπ᾿ ἀριθμόν 207 Ἐπιστολή του (*Τοῖς κατά Νεοκαισάρειαν Κληρικοῖς*) ὁ ἱερός Πατήρ κάνει λόγο μέ πολύ πόνο γιά τό ἀδικαιολόγητο μῖσος τῶν Νεοκαισαρέων κληρικῶν ἐναντίον του, οἱ ὁποῖοι μέχρις ἑνός ἀκολούθησαν τόν τοπικό ἀρχηγό τοῦ πολέμου ἐναντίον του. Σημειώνει μάλιστα ὅτι ἐνῷ ἤδη ἀπευθύνθηκε σ᾿ αὐτούς μέ γράμμα του, ἐν τούτοις δέν ἀξιώθηκε ἀπαντήσεώς των.

Ἐδῶ ὁ Μ. Βασίλειος εὑρίσκεται ἐνώπιον ἑνός σοβαροῦ προβλήματος ἀνθρωπίνων σχέσεων, τό ὁποῖο ἔχει χαραχτῆρα ἀδιεξόδου διότι δέν ὑπάρχει γραμμή καί σύνδεση ἐπικοινωνίας. Δέν τό ἀντιμετωπίζει ὅμως παθητικά ἀλλά γράφει στούς Νεοκαισαρεῖς κληρικούς μέ παρρησία καί ἀναιρεῖ τίς ἐναντίον του κατηγορίες. Καί το κάνει ὄχι τόσο γιά νά διακαιώσῃ τόν ἑαυτό του ὅσο γιά νά διαλύσῃ τό ψεῦδος καί τήν απάτη καί νά προφυλάξη τούς πιστούς από τήν πλάνη. Γράφει σχετικά:

Ή μέν συμφωνία τοῦ καθ' ἡμῶν μίσους καί τό μέχρις ἑνός πάντας ἀκολουθῆσαι τῷ προεστῶτι τοῦ καθ' ἡμῶν πολέμου ἔπειθέ με ὁμοίως ἀποσιωπᾶν πρός ἅπαντας, καί μήτε γράμματαος φιλικοῦ μήτε τινός ὁμιλίας κατάρχειν, ἀλλ' ἐν ἡσυχίᾳ πέσσειν τήν ἐμαυτοῦ λύπην. Ἐπειδή δέ χρή μήτε πρός τάς διαβολάς ἀποσιωπᾶν, οὐχ ἵνα διά τῆς ἀντιλογίας ἡμᾶς αὐτούς ἐκδικῶμεν, ἀλλ' ἵνα μή συγχωρήσωμεν εὐοδωθῆναι τῷ ψεύδει καί τούς ἠπατημένους μή ἐναφῶμεν τῇ βλάβῃ, ἀναγκαῖον ἐφάνη μοι καί τοῦτο προσθεῖναι τοῖς πᾶσι καί ἐπιστεῖλαι ὑμῶν τῇ συνέσει, εἰ καί ὅτι πρώην κοινῇ παντί τῷ πρεσβυτερίῳ γράψαντες οὐδεμιᾶς παρ' ὑμῶν ἀποκρίσεως ἠξιώθημεν.

Καί καταλήγει: ὅσο ἀναπνέω καί μπορῶ νά μιλήσω δέν εἶναι δυνατόν νά μείνω σιωπηλός ἐνώπιον μιᾶς τέτοιας ἀπειλῆς κατά τῶν ψυχῶν τῶν ἀνθρώπων: «Ἕως ἄν ἐμπνέομεν καί δυνάμεθα φθέγγεσθαι, ἀμήχανον ἡμᾶς ἐπί τοσαύτῃ λύμῃ ψυχῶν σιωπᾶν.»

Γιά τήν μεγάλη ψυχή καί διάνοια τοῦ Μ. Βασιλείου, ἦτο ἀδιανόητο, καί φυσικά ὀδυνηρότατο, τό ὅτι εἰσέπραττε ἀπό τούς κληρικούς τῆς Νεοκαισαρείας πού ευεργέτησε, όχι απλώς αχαριστία, ή, πολύ περισσότερο μίσος, αλλά ωμή άρνηση στοιχειώδους ανθρώπινης επικοινωνίας. Τό αδιέξοδο ήτο σαφές. Αλλά ό Μ. Βασίλειος δέν τό δέχθηκε ώς αδιέξοδο. Δέν υπέκυψε σ' αυτό. Τό είδε ώς πρόβλημα πού έπρεπε νά λυθή. Καί τό έλυσε προχωρώντας μόνος του σ' ένα δύσβατο καί μακρύ δρόμο, γνωρίζοντας ότι τελικά οι αντίπαλοί του θά τόν συναντούσαν αναπόφευκτα σέ κάποιο σημείο, πράγμα πού έγινε.

Ό Άγιος Γρηγόριος ό Θεολόγος καί τά ανθρώπινα αδιέξοδα

Είναι γνωστές οι δραματικές περιπτώσεις αδιεξόδων πού συνάντησε στήν ζωή του τόσο στό προσωπικό επίπεδο όσο καί στό εκκλησιαστικό, ό Άγιος Γρηγόριος ό Θεολόγος. Ή μεγαλοφυής διάνοιά του καί παράλληλα ή ασυνήθης λεπτότητα τής ψυχής του κατέστησαν τά αδιέξοδα πού αντιμετώπισε περισσότερο οδυνηρά. Όπως είπε, επαναλαμβάνοντας τούς λόγους τοϋ Εκκλησιαστού, ό προστιθείς γνώσιν προσθήσει άλγημα. (Έκκλησ. 1,18) Ή βαθειά καί διεισδυτική γνώση τών αδιεξόδων έγινε άλγος καί οδύνη γιά τήν ιδιαίτερα αισθαντική ψυχή του. Αύτή τήν οδύνη τήν εξέφρασε μέ τρόπο αριστουργηματικό σέ πολλά κείμενά του καί ιδιαίτερα στά ποιήματά του, γραμμένα στή γλώσσα τών λυρικών ποιητών τής κλασσικής αρχαίας Ελληνικής γραμματείας. Από τά ποιήματα αυτά αξίζει νά δούμε μερικά αποσπάσματα ενδεικτικά τοϋ τρόπου μέ τόν οποίο περιγράφει καί παράλληλα άντιμετωπίζει τά άνθρώπινα άδιέξοδα. Πρέπει βεβαίως νά διευκρινισθῇ ὅτι ὅταν ὁ Ἅγιος Γρηγόριος ὁμιλεῖ στά ποιήματά του σέ πρῶτο πρόσωπο δέν ἐννοεῖ ἀπαραιτήτως καί μόνο τόν ἑαυτό του. Ὅπως ὁ Ἀπόστολος Παῦλος στό ἕβδομο κεφάλαιο τῆς πρός Ρωμαίους Ἐπιστολῆς του ὁμιλεῖ γενικά καί ἐξ ὀνόματος τοῦ κάθε ἀνθρώπου, ἔστω καί ἄν χρησιμοποιεῖ πρῶτο πρόσωπο, ἔτσι καί ὁ Γρηγόριος στά ποιήματα του. Ἄς προχωρήσουμε ὅμως σέ μερικά συγκεκριμένα παραδείγματα.

Κάνει ἀμέσως ἐντύπωση ὅτι στά 98 ποιήματά του πού ἀνήκουν στήν κατηγορία τῶν ἱστορικῶν ποιημάτων τά 20 ἔχουν ὡς τίτλο τήν λέξη «θρῆνος» ἤ κάτι παρόμοιο ὅπως «θρηνητικόν» ἤ «ἐλεγειακόν» ἤ «ἐπιτάφιος». Ποιά ἀκριβῶς ἀδιέξοδα περιγράφονται στά κείμενα αὐτά;

Τό πρῶτο εἶναι ἡ γενική ἀνθρώπινη κατάσταση βαθμιαίας φθορᾶς, ματαιότητος καί ριζικῆς ἀλλοτριώσεως. Γράφει στό ὑπ' ἀριθμόν 43 ποίημά του:

Ποῦ εἶναι τά λόγια τά φτερωτά; Στόν ἀέρα.
Ποῦ εἶναι τῆς νεότητός μου τό ἄνθος; Χάθηκε.
Ποῦ εἶναι ἡ δόξα; Ἄφαντη ἔγινε.
Ποῦ εἶναι τό σθένος τῶν ρωμαλέων μελῶν
 τοῦ σώματος; Τό ἔκαμψε ἡ ἀρρώστια.
Ποῦ εἶναι τά κτήματα καί ὁ πλοῦτος;
 Ἔχει Θεός.
Ἄλλα πράγματα; Τά ρήμαξαν τά
 ἁρπακτικά χέρια τοῦ φθόνου.

Οἱ δέ γονεῖς καί ἡ ἱερή δυάδα τῶν ἀδελφῶν
σέ τάφο πῆγαν.
Μόνη μοῦ ἔμεινε ἡ πατρίδα, ἀλλά καί ἀπ'
αὐτήν μέ ἔδιωξε ὁ κακοῦργος δαίμων.
Καί τώρα ξένος, ἔρημος, βρίσκομαι σέ
ἀλλότρια γῆ σέρνοντας βίο θλίψεων
καί γηρατειά ἀνίσχυρα, ἄθρονος,
ἄπολις, ἄπαις πηγή, γιά τούς γεννήτορες,
ζώντας ἡμέρα μέ τήν ἡμέρα σέ
ἀέναη περιπλάνηση.
Ποῦ θά ρίξω αὐτό τό σῶμα;
Ποιό τέλος θά μέ βρεῖ;
Ποιά γῆ καί ποιός φιλόξενος τάφος θά
μέ σκεπάσει;
Χριστέ βασιλεῦ, ἐσύ εἶσαι ἡ πατρίδα μου,
ἡ δύναμή μου, ὁ πλοῦτος μου, τά πάντα.
Γι' αὐτό καί σέ Σένα θά βρῶ ἀναψυχή
ἀφήνοντας τόν βίο καί τά παρόντα.

Τά ἴδια βιώματα ἐκφράζονται καί στό ὑπ' ἀριθμόν 74 ποίημα:

Γιατί αὐτή ἡ τυραννία; Ἦλθα στή
ζωή· καλῶς.
Γιατί στροβιλίζομαι μέσα στίς τρικυμίες
τοῦ βίου;
Θά πῶ κάτι πού εἶναι θρασύ· ἀλλά
θά τό πῶ.
Ἐάν δέν ἤμουν δικός Σου, Χριστέ μου,
ἔχω ἀδικηθεῖ.

Γεννιόμαστε, διαλυόμεθα, ἐξαντλούμεθα,
ὑπνῶ, καθεύδω, γρηγορῶ, πορεύομαι,
ἀσθενοῦμε, ὑγιαίνουμε, ἡδονές, πόνοι.
Γεννηθήκαμε γιά νά μετέχουμε στή
λάμψη τοῦ ἡλίου, ἐνῶ ὅταν πεθαίνουμε
ἡ σάρκα μας σαπίζει στή γῆ· αὐτά
συμβαίνουν καί στά ἀσήμαντα ζῶα, τά
ὁποῖα ὅμως εἶναι ἀνεύθυνα.
Λοιπόν, τί περισσότερο ἔχω;
Τίποτε παρά μόνο τόν Θεό.
Ἐάν δέν ἤμουν δικός Σου, Χριστέ μου,
ἔχω ἀδικηθεῖ.

Ἐδῶ ὅμως, εἰσάγεται καί ἡ ἔννοια μιᾶς ἀδικίας τήν ὁποία ὑφίσταται ὁ ἄνθρωπος, ἔννοια ἡ ὁποία ἐκφράζεται ἔντονα στή φράση πού ἐπαναλαμβάνεται δύο φορές σέ δώδεκα στίχους-γραμμές: «Εἰ μή σός ἤμην ἠδίκημαι Χριστέ μου.» Ἡ ἴδια ἰδέα διατυπώνεται καί πάλι ἀλλά μέ διαφορετικές ἀναφορές καί συσχετίσεις στό ὑπ' ἀριθμόν 33 ποίημα:

Ἀλίμονό μου, κουράστηκα Χριστέ μου,
πνοή τῶν θνητῶν.
Ἀλίμονό μου, βλέπω μάχη καί ζάλη.
Ἀλίμονό μου, ἀντιμετωπίζω μακρά ζωή
καί παροικία στή γῆ, γεμάτη μέ πταίσματα ἔνδοθεν καί ἔξωθεν ἀπό τά
ὁποῖα φθείρεται τό κάλλος τῆς θείας
εἰκόνος.
Ποιά δρῦς ὑπομένει τέτοια βία ἀνέμων;

Ποιό καράβι χτυπήθηκε ἀπό τόσα κύματα;
Μέ διαπερνάει ὁ πόνος, οἱ ἐπιδρομές
τῶν πραγμάτων τοῦ κόσμου . . .
Οἱ φίλοι μέ γονάτισαν, ἡ ἀρρώστια
μέ ἔφθειρε.
Ἐδέχθηκα λιθοβολισμούς ὅπως οἱ ἄλλοι
δέχονται ἄνθη.
Χωρίστηκα ἀπό τό λαό τόν ὁποῖο τό
Ἅγιο Πνεῦμα ἵδρυσε.
Ὅσο γιά τά τέκνα, μερικά τά ἄφησα,
μερικά μέ ἐγκατέλειψαν, ἀπό μερικά
δέν ἔχω τιμηθεῖ. Ὦ πατρός παναθλίου!
Οἱ ἀδελφοί μου κληρικοί πιό δυσμενεῖς
ἀπ' τούς ἐχθρούς δέν ἔχουν φόβο οὔτε
ἐνώπιον τῆς Ἁγίας Τραπέζης ἄν ὄχι
τίποτε ἄλλο ἀκόμη καί πονηροί ἄνθρωποι
συνηθίζουν νά τιμοῦν κάτι πού ἀποτελεῖ καθιερωμένο ἔθος . . . ἀλλ' οἱ
ἐχθροί μου σ' ἕνα μόνο ἀποβλέπουν,
στήν ἀτίμωσή μου.

Ἐδῶ τό ἀδιέξοδο πλήν τῆς γενικῆς ἀνθρώπινης καταστάσεως ἐπεκτείνεται καί σέ ζητήματα ἀνθρωπίνων συγκρούσεων ὀδυνηρῶν καί δυσεπιλήτων. Στό ἴδιο ποίημα ὁ Ἅγιος Γρηγόριος εἰσάγει τήν ἔννοια τῆς θείας εἰκόνος πού εἶναι ὁ ἄνθρωπος. Μιᾶς εἰκόνος τήν ὁποία βλέπει νά φθείρεται λόγω ἀρνητικῶν ἀνθρωπίνων συνθηκῶν καί συγκρούσεων. Γι' αὐτό καί θρηνεῖ στό ποίημα ὑπ' ἀριθμόν 61:

Ἡ εἰκών κενοῦται, τίς βοηθήσει λόγος;
Ἡ εἰκών κενοῦται, δῶρον ἀχράντου Θεοῦ.
Ὑβρίζεται ἡ εἰκών· καίομαι, ὦ φθόνε,
φθόνε μέ ξένους λόγους καί σοφίσματα.

Ἐδῶ ὅμως βλέπει κάποιο διέξοδο:

Πηγή κακῶν μή ἀνάβλυζε, διάνοια μή
γίνεσαι ματαία.
Καί σύ γλῶσσα μή δέχεσαι τόν βόρβορο.
Καί σύ χέρι μή δέχεσαι τά χειρότερα.
Ἔτσι ἡ εἰκόνα μας θά μείνει ἄφθαρτη.
Οὕτως ἄν εἰκών ἡμῖν ἄφθαρτος μένῃ.

Σέ ὅλες τίς παραπάνω περιπτώσεις πού σταχυολογήσαμε μεταξύ πολλῶν, τό ἀδιέξοδο εἶναι ἡ ἀνθρώπινη κατάσταση πού ὀφείλεται τόσο στήν φύση καί οὐσία τοῦ ἀνθρώπου ὅσο καί στό ἐγκόσμιο κακό. Ποιά εἶναι ἡ πρόταση-λύση τοῦ Ἁγίου Γρηγορίου; Τήν διατυπώνει ἐπιγραμματικά σέ ἕνα ἀπό τά ὡραιότερα ποιήματά του, μέ τίτλο *Περί τοῦ ἐπικήρου τῆς ἀνθρωπίνης φύσεως*.

Τό ποίημα ἀρχίζει μέ τήν θέση ἑνός ἀκραίου ἐρωτήματος. Γράφει ὁ Γρηγόριος:

Ἐγώ καί ὁ χρόνος, ὅπως τά πουλιά ἤ τά
καράβια στό πέλαγος ἀντιπαρερχόμεθα
ἀλλήλους μή ἀφήνοντας πίσω μας
τίποτα πού νά μένει.
Σέ ὅ,τι ὅμως ἔχουμε ἐμπλακεῖ δέ φεύγει

ἀλλά μένει· πρᾶγμα κουραστικότατο
γιά τή ζωή.
Δέν ξέρω καί τί νά προσευχηθῶ;
νά ἐξακολουθήσω νά ζῶ ἤ νά πεθάνω;
Καί στίς δύο περιπτώσεις μέ καταλαμβάνει τρόμος.

Τό μεγάλο ἐρώτημα εἶναι «δέν ξέρω καί τί νά προσευχηθῶ; νά ἐξακολουθήσω νά ζῶ ἤ νά πεθάνω;». Ἀλλά στό τέλος τοῦ ἴδιου ποιήματος, λίγους στίχους παρακάτω ἀπαντᾶ: «Τί θά ποῦμε; Ἕνα εἶναι τό ἄριστο, τό νά ἀτενίζουμε πρός Σέ τό Θεό μόνον καί πρός τήν μεγαλόδωρη ἀγάπη σου.» Γιά τόν Γρηγόριο ὁ Θεός εἶναι ἡ λύση τοῦ ὑπαρξιακοῦ καί κάθε ἀδιεξόδου. Δέν εἶναι τυχαῖο ὅτι ἡ τελική στροφή πρός τόν Θεό ὡς τήν μόνη λύση, διατυπώνεται σέ δεύτερο πρόσωπο, δηλαδή, σέ σχέση ἀμέσου κοινωνίας μεταξύ τοῦ ἀνθρωπίνου ἐγώ καί τοῦ θείου Σύ.

Τό ἴδιο φαινόμενο τῆς τελικῆς στροφῆς πρός τόν Θεό παρατηρεῖται σταθερά στά ποιήματα τοῦ Γρηγορίου. Συγκεκριμένα, στά κείμενα πού ἀναφέραμε σήμερα συναντοῦμε κατά σειρά τίς ἀκόλουθες καταλήξεις.

Στό πρῶτο ποίημα:

Χριστέ βασιλεῦ, ἐσύ εἶσαι ἡ πατρίδα μου,
ἡ δύναμή μου, ὁ πλοῦτος μου, τά πάντα.
Γι' αὐτό καί σέ Σένα θά βρῶ ἀναψυχή
ἀφήνοντας τόν βίο καί τά παρόντα.

Στό δεύτερο:

> Λοιπόν, τί περισσότερο ἔχω;
> Τίποτε παρά μόνο τόν Θεό.
> Ἐάν δέν ἤμουν δικός Σου, Χριστέ μου,
> ἔχω ἀδικηθεῖ.

Ἡ ἔντονη στροφή πρός τόν Θεό μεταμορφώνει ἀκόμη καί τό στοιχεῖο τῆς ἀδικίας.

Στό τρίτο κείμενο ἡ πρός τόν Θεό στροφή εἶναι στήν ἀρχή ὄχι στό τέλος τοῦ ποιήματος:

> Ἀλίμονο, κουράστηκα Χριστέ μου,
> πνοή τῶν θνητῶν . . . .

Ὅ,τι ἀκολουθεῖ πρέπει νά διαβασθῆ ὑπό τό φῶς τοῦ ἀρχικοῦ αὐτοῦ στίχου πού ἔχει ἔντονο χαρακτῆρα προσωπικῆς σχέσεως καί ἐλπίδος («Χριστέ μου, πνοή τῶν θνητῶν»). Πρέπει νά σημειωθῆ ὅτι σέ τελική ἀνάλυση τά ποιήματα τοῦ Ἁγίου Γρηγορίου εἶναι προσευχές. Γι' αὐτό καί οἱ δραματικές περιγραφές ἀδιεξόδων δέν εἶναι ἐκφράσεις ἀπελπισίας ἀλλά προσπάθειες συσχετίσεως τῶν ἀδιεξόδων μέ τόν Θεό ὡς τήν μόνη ρεαλιστική σταθερή καί βιώσιμη λύση. Ἀπό τήν ἄποψη αὐτή ὁμοιάζουν μέ τούς Ψαλμούς τοῦ Δαυΐδ, πού συνδυάζουν ἐξαιρετικά τολμηρή γλῶσσα στήν περιγραφή τῶν δεινῶν καί τῶν συμφορῶν μέ γλῶσσα ἀπόλυτης ἐμπιστοσύνης καί πίστεως σέ ἕνα Θεό πού αἴρει τά ἀδιέξοδα.

Ἐπιλογικά

Ἡ ἐποχή μας εἶναι ἐποχή φορτωμένη μέ ἀδιέξοδα καί πολύπλοκα προβλήματα. Ὁ χῶρος ἀκριβῶς αὐτός ἀνήκει σέ μιά γῆ ἱερή πού ἐπί αἰῶνες μακρούς γνώρισε καί γνωρίζει ὀδυνηρά ἀδιέξοδα στό προσωπικό, τό κοινωνικό καί τό ἐθνικό ἐπίπεδο. Στό σημεῖο αὐτό οἱ Μεγάλοι Πατέρες τῆς Ἐκκλησίας μποροῦν κάλλιστα νά εἶναι ὁδηγοί μας. Διότι ὡμίλησαν καί ἔγραψαν μέ πάθος καί πειστικότητα γιά τίς δυνατότητες ἐξόδου ἀπό τό ἀδιέξοδο. Δυνατότητες πού θά μποροῦσαν νά συμπυκνωθοῦν σέ δύο φράσεις:

Ἡ πρώτη ἀπό τόν Ἅγιο Ἰωάννη τόν Χρυσόστομο: «*Πιστεῦσαι δεῖ ὅτι τά ἀδύνατα δύναται Θεός*», καί ἡ δεύτερη ἀπό τόν Μέγα Βασίλειο: «*Ὅσο ἀναπνέουμε καί μποροῦμε νά μιλοῦμε εἶναι ἀδύνατο νά μείνουμε σιωπηλοί ἐνώπιον τοῦ κινδύνου καταστροφῆς τῶν ἀνθρωπίνων ὑπάρξεων.*»

Human Impasses
and the Church Fathers

University of Cyprus
January 26, 2006

Translated by Pavlos Gottfried

Introduction

Throughout the world's existence, human impasses of every kind that allow for no solution have always been, are now, and will continue to be an integral part of human life—one that is painful, but inescapable. The inevitability of these dead-end situations is due, in essence, to the nature of human existence and the human condition. Existential philosophers of the twentieth century, such as Martin Heidegger, Karl Jaspers, and Jean-Paul Sartre—and before them Sören Kierkegaard—spoke at length and in great detail about what have been called boundary conditions of human existence: pain, anxiety, guilt, and death. For existential philosophers, these impasse situations cannot be surmounted, which is why they were said to be boundary conditions of human existence. It is precisely because of these insurmountable conditions which we confront both as individuals and as social beings—pain, anxiety, guilt, and death—that human beings unavoidably and inevitably find themselves face to face with impassable difficulties of every form and significance.

Long before the time of the existential philosophers, the Church Fathers had in effect described the conditions of human existence that result in impasse. They did so in an unparalleled fashion, albeit using very different language and terminology. They spoke about *the sin that clings so closely* (Heb. 12:1), about worldly evil, and about the tragedy of human mortality. For the Church Fathers, these three things—sin, evil, and mortality, all three co-existing in close association—inexorably and in an almost deterministic way, bring about the unbelievable series of dead-end situations that human beings face. These insurmountable stalemates involve personal, social, and national concerns; furthermore, they have a direct and powerful influence on entire populations.

The Church Fathers spoke and wrote both extensively and in depth about these conditions of human impasse; in a deeply moving way, they expressed their grief over the hardship and affliction that human beings suffer when facing these stalemate situations and these intractable problems. At the same time, however, the great Fathers wrote and spoke passionately, as well as persuasively, not only about the possibility and the means to transcend these impasse situations but also about the potential for conquering the problems that arise from them.

Allow me to present here, very briefly, some specific examples that the Fathers offer in their writings of various types of human impasse and how these situations can be transcended. I will limit myself to the works of the three greatest patristic figures: St. John Chrysostom, St. Basil the Great, and St. Gregory the Theologian. These three outstanding luminaries and ecumenical teachers offer us an immense wealth of material on the present subject. Furthermore, the fact that their feast day is approaching, the feast of the Three Hierarchs, makes our examination of their writings even more timely. Needless to say, the examples from patristic writings in the following discussion have been selected from an enormous wealth and variety of material. Obviously, therefore, only a limited number of such passages could be included; the selections that follow are simply a sample of characteristic passages.

Saint John Chrysostom and the Human Impasses

For Chrysostom, a central and persistent component of impasse is humankind's hopelessly low moral and ethical condition. In his fourth homily of his commentary on *The Gospel According to Matthew*, the holy Father addresses his remarks to human beings in this age of the Fall and of sin, and he uses extremely vivid language to describe the abysmal profundity of our ethical inferiority and corruption. To such a human being, Chrysostom says with profound pain:

> Nor can I even discern clearly whether
> you are a human being, when you kick

like an ass, or bound like a bull . . . or satiate yourself like a bear, or indulge your flesh like a mule, when you are spiteful like a camel, prey like a wolf, burn with anger like a serpent, strike like a scorpion, and are deceitful like a fox, or when you harbor the poison of wickedness like an asp or a viper or make war against your brothers like that wicked demon. How will I be able to count you among the ranks of men, if I do not see in you the marks of such a nature? What should I call you? An animal? Animals possess only one of these faults, but by gathering them all together, you far exceed an animal's brutishness. Should I call you a demon? A demon, however, is neither a slave to the tyranny of his stomach, nor is he in love with wealth. Since you have more faults than both beasts and demons, tell me, how can I call you a human being? Indeed, even more grievous is the fact that, being in such a bad condition, we do not even grasp how our soul has no form, nor do we perceive its ugliness. For not only is our soul formless, it has even taken an animal-shaped form—yet we do not perceive this, not even a little.
(*Fourth Homily* on The Gospel According to Matthew, Migne P.G. 57, 48-49)

His rhetorical exaggeration aside, Chrysostom eloquently describes a situation in which the level of morality is hopelessly low, as is the more general quality of being human. At every step he emphasizes that these situations, on both the personal as well as the social plane, are genetic of an impasse and that they give rise to chronic problems inside families, heated conflicts between social groups, and bloody wars between nations. At first view, these circumstances would seem to have reference only to individuals; but it is clear, due to the kind of problems they are, that they have heavy consequences for society at large.

How does Chrysostom confront these circumstances, which are unquestionably the most serious problems of our existence and which often present us with deadlock situations?

A simplified and extremely condensed look at his views on this subject would focus on two central positions that he believes can transform these stalemate situations into problems that can be solved and transcended. Chrysostom develops the first of these views with particular emphasis in his commentary on St. Paul's letter *To the Romans*. His view is that such impasses can be transcended through faith in God. For Chrysostom, faith provides the only possibility that human beings have to transform themselves and the deadlock situations they face. It must of course be said that for St. John Chrysostom, faith is not simply a religious state of mind, nor is it a phenomenon that suggests passivity, laziness, escapism, weakness, or intellectual inertia. Quite the contrary, faith is an expression of strength, wisdom, and a nobility of soul which radiates the truth that "God can do the impossible." (*Eighth Homily*, To the Romans, Migne P.G. 60, 455)

In order to make this point absolutely clear and to dispel all doubts, the holy Father speaks at length about Abraham, a dominant figure in the fourth chapter of St. Paul's letter *To the Romans*. He persuasively demonstrates that Abraham's faith before the dreadful impasse he faced was an expression "of his exceedingly noble soul, his philosophical mind, and his lofty intellect. For not stealing and not murdering are things one meets with every day, but believing that God is able to do the impossible requires a genius and noble soul that is also exceedingly drawn toward God." (*Eighth Homily*, To the Romans, Migne P.G. 60, 455)

This is the point where Chrysostom boldly formulates his certainty about the nobility and the genius of faith and its absolute ability to lead human beings from a state of impasse to the gateway of salvation. Certainly, the radical change of human conditions through faith is, in the final analysis, the work of God in the person of Jesus Christ. On this point Chrysostom writes:

> Even if you are a Gentile, even if you practice every evil habit, even if you are a Scythian, a barbarian, a very beast, filled with unreasonableness and bearing the burden of a thousand sins, even then, if you have accepted the word of the Cross

> and were baptized, you have erased all those things. . . . For in this God's justice is revealed. . . . Moreover, justice is not yours, but God's, and he [Paul] hints at how abundant and how easy it is. For you do not achieve it through sweat and labor; you receive it as a gift from above if you contribute just one thing: your faith. (*Second Homily*, To the Romans Migne P.G. 60, 408–9)

The second point on which Chrysostom insists in every one of his works is the possibility of transcending impasse through the decisive contribution of that human element which in Greek is called *proairesis*. For Chrysostom, *proairesis* means free choice, a deliberate and intentional choice, a free decision. This word was already familiar from the classical tradition, through Plato and Aristotle (see Plato, *Parmenides*, 143C; Aristotle, *Politics*, 1280a34), as well as through a number of older ecclesiastical writers that preceded Chrysostom, such as Justin Martyr, Clement of Alexandria, Tatian, Origen, Athansius the Great, and Gregory of Nyssa. (See Justin Martyr, *Dialogue with Tryphon*, 88, 5; Clement of Alexandria, *The Stromata*, 4–5; Tatian, *To the Greeks*, 7; Origen, *De Principiis*, 3.1.24; Athansius the Great, *Treatise on the Incarnation of the Word*, P.G. 25, 101C; and Gregory of Nyssa, *The Great Catechism*, P.G. 45, 77A.)

In Chrysostom, however, and particularly in his commentary on St. Paul's letter *To the Romans*, the word *proairesis* is a very frequently used term that implies a combination of elements having to do with the will, the intellect, and the emotions. For Chrysostom, *proairesis* is at the core of a human being, is a fundamental and inalienable distinguishing characteristic, and is the substantive heart of our true identity. From a human standpoint, *proairesis* provides the element that we require to transform our individual selves and to radically change our problems and our circumstances of impasse. In order to emphasize the decisive importance of *proairesis*, the holy Father uses the example of a precious and unbreakable stone, like a diamond. In this regard he writes:

> Do you not see the diamond resist when it is struck? But it has this ability, you will say, from nature. Yet it is also possible for you to be this strong, by virtue of your *proairesis*, in the very same way that this occurs, from nature, for the diamond. (*Third Homily*, To the Romans Migne P.G. 60, 416)

Proairesis can even change nature itself; that is, it can change the naturally occurring givens of human existence, such as those stalemate situations. For Chrysostom, it is the synergy of human *proairesis* and divine power that provides us with the certainty to confront dead-end situations of every kind.

Saint Basil the Great and the Human Impasses

In his eventful and extraordinary life, St. Basil the Great found himself facing a host of no-way-out situations that covered an extremely wide range of issues. These included issues concerning faith, learning, ecclesiastical position, and human behavior, as well as personal and social issues, tormenting illnesses, unjust exiles, and bitter deaths. On reading his masterly writings, one gets a picture of the host of problems that he met at every step—problems that in many instances were truly prohibiting impasses.

In his letters, for instance, St. Basil throws into relief the great problems and deadlocks he faced. Examples of this are scattered throughout his 368 surviving letters, whose personal character makes them even more revealing of the impasse situations this great fighter for faith, truth, and human dignity had to overcome.

In this regard, one could cite two characteristic examples.

The first involves the tragic impasse that was created in the Churches as a result of the madness and stupor of the heresies. He writes about this in Letter 90, *To Our Most Holy Brothers, the Bishops in the West*:

> For the Church here is now worn out, most honored brethren, and is attacked by the constant assaults of its adversaries, like some ship at sea that continues to be pounded by wave upon wave, un-

less there is some sudden visitation of the Lord's loving-kindness .... Our afflictions are well-known, even if we do not speak of them; word of them has spread throughout the world. The doctrines of the Fathers are disdained; apostolic traditions are counted for nothing; and theories of the young hold sway in our Churches, where men engage in sophistry rather than theology. Worldly wisdom is held in first place, and the glory of the Cross is rejected. Shepherds are driven away and replaced by heavy wolves, who scatter Christ's flock. Houses of prayer are bereft of churchgoers, and the deserts are full of those who cry out in grief. The elders mourn when they compare the past with the present; the young are to be pitied, since they don't know what has been taken from them.

The holy Father returns to this theme in Letter 92, *To the Italians and the Gauls*, where he writes:

> This danger does not just threaten the one, two, or three churches that have met with this terrible storm. The evil of this heresy spreads almost from the borders of Illyria to the Thebaid. Its wicked seeds were first sown by that evil name, Arius.

Since that time, through the diligent care of the many who cultivate ungodliness, these seeds have sunk deep roots and have now borne their destructive fruit. The doctrines of piety have been overturned, and the laws of the Church have been thrown into confusion. . . . Priestly piety is a thing of the past; there is a total lack of men who can shepherd the Lord's flock with knowledge; and ambitious men squander the portion that belongs to the poor on their own personal enjoyment and on the distribution of gifts. Accuracy regarding the Church's canons has disappeared, and the license to sin is great. . . . Lawful judgment has utterly vanished, and everyone does whatever they want. Wickedness has increased without measure, the people are ungovernable, and their leaders are not free to speak. . . . There can be no truce in this conflict, since those who perpetuate the evil deeds view public order with suspicion, thinking it will reveal their shameful secrets. The faithless laugh at these things, and those whose faith is weak are shaken. Faith is in doubt and ignorance is sown in peoples' souls. . . . The mouths of the pious are silent, but the tongue of every blasphemer is let loose.

Holy things have been profaned, and those whose faith remains strong shun our houses of prayer as schools of impiety. But out in the desert, with heavy sighs and tears, they lift their hands toward our Lord in heaven.

In Letter 243, *To the Bishops of Italy and Gaul Concerning the Condition and Confusion of the Churches*, he adds:

Persecution [due to heresies] has overtaken us, most honored brethren, and it is the most grievous of persecutions. Shepherds are persecuted in order to scatter their flocks.... The sound of people's lamentations can be heard in the city, in the fields, on the roads, and in the deserts. All those lamenting have one piteous voice. Joy and spiritual gladness have been snatched away, and our feasts have been turned into mourning. Our houses of prayer have been closed, and the altars of our spiritual worship lay unused. No longer are there gatherings of Christians, no longer do our teachers hold a place of authority. Lessons for salvation are not heard. There are no festivals. There is no singing of hymns through the night. Nor is there that blessed spiritual rejoicing in our souls—in our assemblies, and in our communion of spiritual gifts—which takes place in the souls of those who believe in the Lord. It is fitting for us to say that "At this time there is no prince, or prophet, or leader, no burnt offering, or sacrifice, or oblation, or incense, no place to make an offering before you or to find mercy." (Daniel 3:38, The Prayer of Azariah 1:15).

In view of these terrifying circumstances of impasse, St. Basil stresses with all his strength that in order to conquer them there is an urgent need for intense belief in God, an increase in fortitude and hope, and perseverance in prayer and in struggle for the word of truth that the Church possesses. In the very place where falsehood and error are sown, St. Basil cries out, sow the truth that sets you free. Where the mouths of the impious "say worthless things" and open incurable wounds, speak of God's justice and love.

In his letters to all the Churches, the holy Father summons them to vigilance and continuous struggle. He writes tirelessly and offers strong arguments to those who struggle to conquer the stalemate situations that heresy and error had created.

The second example which deserves some brief mention has to do with a different kind of impasse, one whose character is personal. In Letter 207, *To the Clergy of Neocaesarea*, the holy Father speaks with great pain about the unjustifiable hatred that the clergy of Neocaesarea have for him. All of them, down to the last, had followed their local leader in his war against St. Basil, who indeed notes that while he had already addressed them by letter, yet he had not been blessed with a response.

Here, St. Basil finds himself facing a serious problem of human relationships, a problem that has the character of an impasse because there exists no link, no line of communication. Nevertheless, he is not passive in the way he deals with this, but writes to the clergy of Neocaesarea with boldness and refutes the accusations against him. Furthermore, he does this not so much as to vindicate himself, but more to dispel falsehood and deception, in order to protect the faithful from error. In this regard he writes:

> Your agreement in your hatred of me and the fact that down to a man you follow your leader in his war against me persuaded me to maintain my silence to all and neither to begin a friendly letter nor to initiate any conversation, but to nurse my own pain in silence. But we should not be silent in the face of slander, not for the purpose of avenging ourselves, but in order that we not allow falsehood to succeed nor permit those deceived to fall into harm. It therefore seemed necessary to me to present this to you and to send

> all of you a letter, even though when I recently wrote to the council of elders as a whole I was not deemed worthy of your reply.

And he concludes:

> As long as I breathe and am able to speak, it is not possible for me to remain silent before such a menace to people's souls.

For the great soul and intellect of St. Basil, it was inconceivable, and of course extremely distressing, that the clergy of Neocaesarea, to whom he had been generous, had repaid him not only with ingratitude, or even worse, with hatred, but with an insensitive refusal to have simple human contact. The deadlock was clear. Nevertheless, St. Basil did not accept it as a deadlock. He saw it as a problem that one should attempt to solve. And he solved it by proceeding alone, on a long and bumpy road, since he recognized that inevitably, at some point, his rivals would encounter him—an event which did take place.

Saint Gregory the Theologian and the Human Impasses

The dramatic impasse situations that St. Gregory the Theologian encountered in his life, on both the personal and ecclesiastical levels, are well known. The genius of his intellect, together with his unusual delicacy of feeling, only increased the painfulness of facing those dead-end situations. As he said, quoting the author of *Ecclesiastes*, "*The one who adds knowledge adds pain*" (1:18). For his particularly sensitive soul, such profound and penetrating understanding of these impasse situations became grief and sorrow. He was a master at expressing this grief in his many writings, particularly in his poetry, which he wrote in the language of the lyric poets of classical ancient Greek literature. It would be valuable for us to look at certain passages from his poems, in which he describes situations of human impasse and at the same time confronts them.

It is of course necessary to clarify that when St. Gregory speaks in his poetry in the first person, he is not necessarily referring only to himself. What St. Gregory does in his poems is what St. Paul does in the seventh chapter of his letter *To the Romans*; namely, he is speaking in general, in the name of every human being, even though he uses the first person singular. Let us now proceed with St. Gregory's texts.

One is immediately impressed by the fact that of his 98 poems that fall into the category of historical poems, twenty of them bear the title "Lament" or something similar, such as "Threnody," "Elegy," or "Epitaph." What exactly are the impasse situations described in these works?

The first is the general human condition of gradual deterioration, futility, and profound alienation. He writes in Poem 43:

Where are my winged words? In the air.
Where is the flower of my youth? Lost.
Where is my splendor? It has become invisible.
Where is the strength of my bodily limbs?
  Bent over with disease.
Where are my wealth and riches to be found?
They belong to God.
But the objects themselves?
  Dashed by the rapacious hands of envy.
My parents and two holy brothers lie
  in their graves.
The only thing left me was my native land,
  but even from there that villainous demon
  has banished me.
Now I'm a stranger, alone, in a strange land
  with a life of afflictions, bearing impotent
  old age in tow, no bishop's throne, no city,
  no children, a source for fathers, living day
  by day in endless wandering.
Where will I cast this body?
What end will find me?
What land, what welcoming grave will
  cover me?
Christ O king, you are my homeland, my
  strength, my wealth, my everything.
In You, therefore, will I find comfort,
  setting aside this life and present matters.

The same experiences are expressed in Poem 74:

> Why this torment?
> I came into life—all well and good.
> But why am I whirled about in these
>   raging storms of life?
> I'll say something audacious—but I'll say it:
> Were I not yours, my Christ, then I have
>   been treated unjustly.
> We are born, we wear down, we give out;
> I sleep, I lie motionless, I become alert,
>   I go forward; we fall ill, we are healthy,
>   we feel pleasure, we feel pain.
> We were born to share in the glow of the sun,
>   but when we die, our flesh decays in the
>   earth; this also happens to insignificant
>   animals, but they don't have to account
>   for themselves.
> So what do I have more? Nothing, except God.
> Were I not yours, my Christ, then I have
>   been treated unjustly.

Here the notion is introduced of an injustice that humanity suffers, and this notion is boldly expressed in the phrase that occurs twice within twelve lines of verse: "Were I not yours, my Christ, then I have been treated unjustly." This same idea is expressed again, but with different allusions and associations, in Poem 33:

> Woe is me, I am tired, O my Christ,
>   the breath of mortals.
> Woe is me, I see struggle and bewilderment.
> Woe is me, I face a long as a stranger on earth,
>   a life filled with sins, inside and out—sins
>   that ravage the beauty of our divine image.
> Does any oak suffer such beating from
>   the winds?
> Has any ship ever been pounded by so
>   many waves?
> Pain penetrates me, the invasions of
>   worldly things....
> My friends have brought me to my knees,
>   illness has destroyed me.
> I received stonings as others receive flowers.
> I have been separated from my people,
>   which was established by the Holy Spirit.
> As to my children, some I left, some
>   abandoned me, and I have not been honored
>   by others. O children of a wretched father!
> My brother clergymen are more hostile than
>   my enemies; they have no fear, not even
>   before the Holy Altar; if nothing else,
>   even wicked men are in the habit of
>   respecting something that constitutes a
>   sanctioned custom. . .but my enemies
>   have only one thing in view, to dishonor me.

At this point, apart from the general human situation, the notion of impasse is extended to include distressing human conflicts that do not allow for easy solutions. In the same poem, St. Gregory introduces the idea of the divine image; namely, that a human being is an image that he sees being corrupted as a result of negative human practices and conflicts. He therefore laments in Poem 61:

> The image is being emptied of its meaning,
>   what words will help?
> The image, a gift of the immaculate God,
>   is emptied of meaning.
> The image is disgraced—I am on fire,
>   O evil one, O envious one, with alien
>   arguments and fallacies.

But here, he sees a way out:

> Wellspring of evils, do not gush forth,
>   intellect do not be without purpose.
> And you, tongue, do not entertain filth.
> And you, hand, do not tolerate the worst things.
> Thus will our image remain incorruptible.
> Thus will our image remain incorruptible.

In all of these examples, which have been gleaned from many, stalemate is the human condition, and it owes as much to the nature and essence of a human being as it does to worldly evil. What solution does St. Gregory propose? He puts it forward succinctly in one of his most beautiful poems, *On Humanity's Perishable Nature*.

The poem begins by posing a radical question. Gregory writes:

> Time and I, like birds or like ships at sea,
> pass each other by, allowing for nothing
> to remain behind us.
> Nevertheless, whatever we have tangled
> with doesn't leave, but remains: a thing
> about life that is extremely tiresome.
> I don't even know what I should pray for—
> to continue to live or to die?
> In both cases, terror seizes me.

The major question is, "I don't know what I should pray for—to continue to live or to die?" But at the end of the same poem, just a few lines below this, he gives his answer: "What should we say? One thing is best, to fix our gaze on You, on God alone, and on your bountiful love." For Gregory, God is the solution to every impasse, existential or otherwise. It is not by chance that he formulates this final turn toward God, the only solution, using the second person—that is, as direct communication between the human "I" and the divine "You."

One constantly observes this ultimate turn toward God in St. Gregory's poems. More specifically, in the three passages quoted above, we have seen, in succession, the following three conclusions:

In the first poem:

> Christ O king, you are my homeland,
>   my strength, my wealth, my everything.
> In You, therefore, will I find comfort,
>   setting aside this life and present matters.

In the second poem:

> So what do I have more?
> Nothing, except God.
> Were I not yours, my Christ,
>   then I have been treated unjustly.

This intense turn toward God even transforms the element of injustice.

In the third passage, the turn toward God is at the beginning of the poem, not at the end:

> Woe is me, I am worn out, O my Christ,
>   the breath of mortals.

Whatever follows should be read in the light of this initial verse, which has the intense character of a personal relationship and of hope (O my Christ, the breath of mortals). It should be noted that in the final analysis, the poems of St. Gregory are prayers. Their vivid descriptions of deadlock situations are therefore not expressions of despair, but are attempts to connect these impasses to

God as the only realistic, constant, and viable solution. Viewed in this way, they resemble the Psalms of David, which combine an exceptionally bold use of language to describe disasters and misfortunes with language that expresses absolute trust and faith in one God who resolves these stalemate situations.

Conclusion

The age we live in is laden with impasses and complex problems. This land (i.e. Cyprus) precisely constitutes a sacred ground, which through long centuries has seen and known painful impasses on the personal, social and national levels. At this point the Great Fathers of the Church can be our best guides. For they spoke and wrote with passion and with persuasiveness about the possibilities for exiting from an impasse—possibilities that could be expressed succinctly in two phrases:

The first is from St. John Chrysostom: *It is necessary to believe that God can do the impossible things*, and the second from St. Basil the Great: *As long as we breathe and are able to speak, it is impossible for us to remain silent in front of the danger of ruin that human beings face.*

Index

A

Abraham 214
Academy of Athens 89
achievements 26, 38, 134, 170, 172
active listening 179
administration 43, 45, 168
Africa 25, 38, 92
Afternoon School 47, 48
aged 31, 64
Age of Reason 96
agnosticism 91
AHEPA 75
alienation 224
ambassadors 17, 20, 27
America 1, 2, 10, 12, 15-16, 19, 20, 23-36, 42-45, 48, 50, 53, 54, 56, 58, 60, 63, 64, 68, 75, 78, 80, 131-134, 136, 142, 144, 145, 146, 149, 151, 152
anathemas 156
Anglican Communion 159
animistic religions 92
anthropology 91, 135
apophaticism 139
Apostles 7, 9, 41, 51, 109, 110-112
Appeal of Conscience Foundation 163
Archbishop Iakovos of North and South America 54
Archbishop Christodoulos of Athens and All Greece 74

Archdiocesan Council 2, 23, 44, 84
Archdiocese 1, 2, 11, 12, 14-16, 20, 22-25, 28, 29, 32, 33, 35, 36, 43-46, 48, 53-57, 59, 60, 61, 66, 69, 71, 73-75, 82
Archons 2, 55, 57, 72
Aristotle 132, 215
art 13, 34, 47, 101
Asia 45, 51
Athansius the Great 215
atheism 91
Augsburg-Constantinople 157
Australia 45
Auxiliary Bishops 22, 56
Azerbaijan 162

B

Bahai Faith 92
Bahrain 162
balance 93, 147-149, 151
Baptism 161
Basil the Great 15, 132, 141, 157, 174, 211, 217, 231
beauty 151, 227
Bible 39, 180
bishops 22, 25, 144, 145
Blaise Pascal 146
blessing 14, 23, 25, 42, 46, 55, 98, 99, 101, 102, 105, 106
blessings 21, 25, 26, 44, 45, 46, 82, 108
boldness 66, 222
brotherhood 92, 115
Buddhism 92

C

canon law 148, 149
catechism 62
Center for Family Care 29, 34
chanting 11, 101
charity 6
Charter 43, 44, 56
children 11, 12, 14, 15, 47, 48, 49, 62, 64, 67, 72, 74, 75, 84, 104, 225, 227
Children's Metropolitan Choir 74
Christendom 162
Christian heritage 155
Christian life 41, 108, 148
Christian martyrdom 170
Christology 148, 150
Church 3-10, 12-17, 22-27, 30, 31, 33-35, 38, 42-46, 48, 50, 51, 54, 55, 57, 58, 60-66, 69, 71, 73-85, 104, 106, 108, 110-113, 117, 132, 133, 135, 138-140, 142-146, 148, 150-152, 158-161, 164, 173, 180, 209, 210, 217, 219, 221, 231
citizen 126, 162
civil liberties 118, 124-125, 129
Clement of Alexandria 134, 215
clergy 2, 12, 24, 29, 44, 55, 69, 74, 98, 115, 145, 148, 170, 222, 223
clergy families 29
commission 19, 26, 27
communication 5, 60, 99, 101, 121, 124, 134, 222, 229
Communications Department 33, 34
communion 79, 113, 115, 158, 221
communities 11, 13, 16, 21, 22, 25, 28, 30-32, 39-40, 42, 43, 46-48, 50, 51, 62, 64, 66, 76, 77, 93, 94, 100, 103, 109, 111-115
community 3, 11-16, 21, 23, 24, 26, 27, 29, 32, 41-43, 48, 50, 65, 76-79, 82, 83, 93, 94, 101, 112, 144, 169, 170
compassion 32, 64, 107, 108, 110-112, 115
completeness 147, 149-151
Confucianism 92
Constantinople 45, 72, 156, 157, 161, 163, 164, 166
cooperation 2, 13, 30, 58, 74, 98, 114, 119, 120, 164
cosmic contest 97, 98
cosmology 91
cosmos 93, 152
counseling 24, 29
Creation 164
creativity 26
crisis 49
Cross 2, 15, 16, 20, 22, 25, 33, 42, 72, 103, 106, 107, 110, 132, 214, 218
cultural education 48
culture 16, 33, 47, 63, 111, 112, 114, 142, 152
Cyprus 72, 74, 209, 231

D

Dark Ages 100
Day School 47
deacons 20, 22
death 8, 20, 21, 23, 24, 69, 103, 105, 106, 109, 112, 145, 209
deception 97, 222
democracy 47
Department of Family and Marriage 29

Department of Religious Education 30
destiny 7, 8
destruction 24, 58, 97, 103
diaconate 22
diaconia 6
dialogue 117-123, 129, 142, 156-165, 173-183
diaspora 77
differentiation 77, 86, 91
dignity 3, 23, 55, 113, 126, 128, 217
Dioceses 11, 28, 32
diseases 38
divine image 227-228
Divine Liturgy 150, 157
Divine Presence 93-99, 102
divorce 29, 48, 49
donors 35

E

ecclesiology 148
economic collapse 115
Ecumenical Councils 8
ecumenical dialogue 156, 157, 158, 160, 162
ecumenical movement 157, 158
Ecumenical Patriarchate 2, 43, 44, 45, 55-57, 72-74, 117, 143, 155-164, 166-171
Ecumenical Patriarch Athenagoras 156, 160
Ecumenical Patriarch Bartholomew 2, 73, 144, 161-164, 181
Ecumenical Patriarch Jeremiah II 158
Ecumenical Patriarch Photios II 158
Ecumenical Synods 9, 140, 180
ecumenism 158

education 12, 34, 46-48, 62, 63, 65, 71, 72, 82, 124, 170
emotions 216
endowment 45
energy 44, 78, 132, 138, 148
English 60, 134-138, 151
environment 38, 112, 113, 133, 157, 164, 165
environmental catastrophes 115
Eparchial Synod 2, 12, 43, 56, 62
Epiphanios 140
equality 113
error 221-222
eschatology 91
ethics 91
ethnicity 85-86
Eucharist 98, 151
Eucharistic 27, 148, 151
Europe 38, 45, 51, 100, 121, 129, 143
European Convention for the Protection of Human Rights and Fundamental Freedoms 126
European Court of Human Rights 72
European Parliament 117, 163
evangelism 43, 50
evil 94, 113, 210, 214, 218, 219, 228
excellence 4, 38, 39, 51, 89, 145

F

faith 4-12, 14-17, 24, 27, 28, 34, 37, 39, 40, 41, 45, 49, 53, 55, 63, 66, 68, 79, 94, 95, 97, 100, 101, 103, 104, 109-114, 115, 125, 127, 128, 132-136, 138-152, 159, 160, 162, 173, 174, 178-180,

213-215, 217, 219, 220, 231
FAITH: An Endowment for Orthodoxy and Hellenism 45
Faith Endowment 46, 47, 58, 71- 73
Fall 211
falsehood 10, 120, 128, 221, 222
families 13, 14, 18, 24, 29, 48, 49, 50, 76, 79, 80, 83, 213
family 13, 14, 29, 38, 43, 48, 49, 50, 58, 61, 63, 79
famine 38
Far East 25, 38
Fathers 8, 9, 62, 132, 140, 141, 155, 209, 210, 218, 231
filioque 161
folk religions 92, 93
force 97, 98, 111, 113, 141, 169
freedom 5, 47, 56, 73, 77, 92, 113, 118-129
free society 124, 125, 128
free will 125
future 3, 6, 12, 26, 47, 63, 67, 101, 102, 110

G

genocide 127
gentleness 6
Gnostics 139, 140
Gnostic sects 92
Gospel 8, 14, 15, 20, 28, 33, 37, 39, 41, 44, 51, 53, 54, 59, 61, 62, 63, 65, 66, 67, 80, 84, 86, 87, 112, 113, 120, 138, 140, 142, 143, 147, 179, 211, 212
governments 113-115
GOYA 30
grace 2, 16, 21, 42, 53, 57, 68, 83, 106, 107, 129, 162, 171

Greece 51, 72-75, 84, 126
Greek 1, 3, 4, 9, 10, 12, 14, 16, 22-26, 30, 33, 35, 44, 50, 53, 56, 58, 63, 64, 72, 76, 77, 78, 82, 85, 96, 132, 134, 135, 137, 149, 152, 162, 167, 169, 170, 215, 224
Greek American 3, 10, 14, 16, 35, 72
Greek American Orthodox Church 10
Greek American Orthodox family 14
Greek Americans 77
Greek Education Department 30
Greek language 63
Greek literature 224
Greek Orthodox Archdiocese 1, 12, 22, 23, 24, 53, 56
Greek Orthodox Church 4, 9, 10, 26, 44, 63
Greek Orthodox Community 23, 76
Greek Orthodox identity 33
Gregory of Nyssa 215
Gregory the Theologian 93, 132, 161, 211, 223
grief 210, 218, 224
growth 7, 21, 27, 28, 30, 31, 33, 35, 71, 73, 75, 94, 148

H

handwriting 141
harmony 93
healing 94, 105, 123, 149, 156, 173, 178
Hellenic College 2, 15, 16, 25, 33, 72, 103
Hellenic heritage 16, 33
Hellenic Orthodox tradition 27

Hellenic tradition 85
Hellenism 45, 47, 71, 72, 77, 83
heresies 217, 220
heresy 218, 221
heritage 10, 16, 33, 48, 111, 115, 155
Hierarchs 2, 20, 22, 45, 56, 132, 211
Hinduism 91
Hippolytos of Rome 139
history 4, 10, 16, 35, 47, 62, 66, 92, 97, 121-123, 128, 134, 145, 148, 155-158, 166, 173, 177, 178
holiness 94, 107
Holy Cross Greek Orthodox School of Theology 15, 22 25, 33, 42, 103, 132
Holy Spirit 8, 41, 150, 151, 156, 162, 171, 227
hubris 96-97
human being 6, 53, 67, 93, 121, 125, 128, 139, 150, 152, 211, 212, 216, 224, 228
human beings 5, 20, 64, 95, 98, 99, 101, 102, 107, 108, 119, 120, 123, 125, 134, 152, 156, 165, 170, 209, 210, 211, 213, 214, 231
human condition 98, 120, 122, 144, 145, 155, 209, 224, 228
human conflicts 228
human consciousness 97
human contact 223
human dialogue 121
human existence 7, 105, 113, 125, 209, 210, 216
human impasse 210, 211, 224
human life 4, 5, 114, 128, 145, 147, 209
human mortality 210

human person 99, 126
human personality 95
human race 97
human relationships 222
human rights 38, 92, 118, 127, 128, 129
human situation 227
human word 180
humanity 8, 19, 91, 97, 100, 106, 112, 114, 123, 125, 134, 226
Hurricane Katrina 57, 58
hymns 110, 134, 137, 138, 220

I

icons 95
identity 216
Ignatius of Antioch 150
immigration 76
impasse 209-231
Incarnation 105, 215
injustice 113, 114, 126, 226, 230
injustices 107, 113, 124
intellect 9, 214, 216, 223-224, 228
intelligence 10
interfaith dialogue 173-179, 181, 183
interfaith families 80
interfaith marriages 29, 77, 80
intermarried family 49, 63
International Orthodox Christian Charities (IOCC) 2, 25, 26, 57
Internet 9, 29, 32
interreligious dialogue 156, 162, 173
Ionian Village 84
Iran 162
Irenaeos 140
Islam 91, 92, 162, 173

J

Jean-Paul Sartre 209
Jesus Christ 6, 8, 17, 20, 26, 44, 53, 61, 62, 66, 68, 86, 87, 104, 110, 138, 142, 143, 150, 152, 171, 172, 179, 182, 214
Jews 77, 100, 156, 162
John Chrysostom 15, 72, 132, 153, 157, 161, 211, 213, 231
joy 3, 8, 53, 55, 63, 68, 71, 82, 106, 131, 141, 152, 184
JOY 30
Judaism 91, 92, 162, 173
Judgment 107, 179, 180
justice 92, 93, 103, 104, 107-115, 122, 127, 162, 215, 221
Justin Martyr 140, 215

K

Karl Jaspers 209
karma 93
kingdom 64, 104, 105, 107, 109 114, 147, 183
knowledge 9, 10, 27, 33, 40, 47, 62, 81, 109, 119, 174, 177, 178, 219, 224

L

Ladies Philoptochos Society 31, 58, 73
laity 12, 24, 43, 60, 98, 145, 148
Lambeth Conference 158-160
language 16, 33, 47, 63, 72, 119, 134-141, 143, 151, 152, 180, 183, 210, 211, 224, 231
Last Supper 105
Latin 134
laws 126, 219
lay 2, 20, 44, 55, 74, 220
Leadership 100 2, 14, 25, 58, 71
learning 9, 34, 80, 100, 119, 174, 175, 179, 217
liberation 101, 120, 145
Libya 162
life 3, 4, 5, 7-13, 17, 20, 21, 26-29, 34, 35, 41, 49, 50, 51, 55, 58, 62, 68, 69, 78, 79, 81, 83, 85, 94, 99, 101, 105, 106, 108-114, 118, 119, 128, 133, 134, 144-148, 156, 172, 209, 217, 223, 225-227, 229, 230
liturgics 148
liturgy 11, 148
love 3, 6, 7, 10, 12, 13, 14, 17, 20, 21, 24, 26, 27, 32, 37, 40-43, 53, 54, 58, 64-67, 81, 101, 102, 105, 106, 107, 109, 110-113, 115, 128, 152, 153, 159, 161, 164, 170-172, 177, 178, 182, 212, 221, 229
Lutheran 158

M

marriage 14, 29, 80, 83, 175
Martin Heidegger 209
martyrs 8, 9, 104, 112, 127, 145, 146
maya 97
meaning 8, 9, 19, 41, 59, 81, 134, 146, 228
media 9, 32, 60, 136
membership 71, 77
memory 21, 24, 55, 70, 71, 74, 100, 101, 102
messengers 17, 20
Metropolises 43, 56, 72, 77, 82, 83, 85

Metropolitans 2, 43, 44
Middle East 38, 57
millennium 3-7, 10, 12, 16, 17
mind 9, 37, 61, 94, 142, 213, 214
ministries 22, 23, 45, 66
ministry 30, 32, 41, 51, 55, 62, 105, 107, 108, 109, 111, 112, 113, 123, 156, 157, 161, 164, 172
mission 7, 20, 33, 44, 51, 53, 57, 63
mixed marriages 14
monotheistic faiths 91, 92
morality 213
Mormonism 92
music 5, 54, 101, 102, 134, 137
Muslims 100, 156, 162
mystery 97, 99, 100, 101

N

National Ministries 15, 71
nations 41, 103, 113, 122, 126, 164, 213
natural disasters 115
natural environment 157, 164, 165
neighborhoods 65, 81
New Testament 39, 72, 109, 127
nobility of soul 214
non-Orthodox 53, 60
North American Orthodox-Catholic Theological Consultation 160

O

Old Testament 127, 183
Olympic Games 38, 83, 89, 90
ordination 43, 55
ordinations 22, 42, 43, 69
Origen 215

Orthodox Campus Fellowship (OCF) 30, 57, 83
Orthodox Christian 25, 39, 57, 83, 98, 162, 168
Orthodox Christian Mission Center (OCMC) 2, 25, 26, 57
Orthodox Christianity 85, 126
Orthodox community 12, 14, 169
Orthodox education 46-48, 62
Orthodox faith 4, 12, 53, 132, 133-136, 138, 140, 142-144, 147-151, 162
Orthodox families 29
Orthodox family 13, 14
Orthodox literature 135
Orthodox parishes 40, 41
Orthodox Patriarchates 158
Orthodox students 30
Orthodox theologians 158
Orthodox tradition 27, 96
Orthodox worship 12, 152
Orthodoxy 30, 35, 36, 45, 47, 58, 60, 63, 64, 71, 72, 83, 131, 132, 134, 135, 145, 146, 148, 150, 152
Orthodoxy in America 60, 131, 152
outreach 43, 50

P

paideia 34
pain 8, 23, 24, 69, 149, 177, 178, 183, 209, 211, 221, 222, 224, 226
pan-Orthodox 57
parable 86, 87
parish 3, 14, 15, 27, 28, 29, 30, 46, 47, 48, 50, 62, 63, 76, 77, 79, 80, 82, 83

parishes 2, 15, 24, 28-35, 40, 41, 42, 46, 48, 50, 62, 64, 80, 82, 87
particularism 91
pastoral theology 148
Patriarch Alexei 74
Patriarchal Theological School 170
Patriarchate of Moscow 74
Patriarch of Alexandria 158, 159
Patristic model 15
Paul 2, 17, 21, 37, 40, 51, 70, 71, 81, 89, 94, 107, 108, 110, 123, 156, 157, 160, 161, 167, 171, 209, 213, 214, 215, 224
peace 20, 51, 55, 92, 94, 103, 104-116, 152, 157, 162, 164
philanthropy 31, 148, 152
Philanthropy Department 31, 34
Philoptochos 2, 13, 31, 58, 64, 73
planning 11, 43, 59, 60
Plato 215
pluralism 119
poetic justice 93
political unrest 115
Pope Benedict XVI 73, 161, 181
Pope John Paul II 161, 167
Pope Paul VI 156, 160
post-modern 96
poverty 38
power 1, 7, 14, 35, 40, 101, 106, 109, 110-113, 156, 168, 171, 180, 183, 184, 216
praxis 148
pray 3, 35, 66, 157, 161, 229
prayer 4, 5, 8, 10, 11, 12, 21, 24, 27, 99, 100, 101, 111, 129, 144, 171, 218, 220, 221

preach 51, 53
presbyteres 55
priesthood 22, 25, 42, 43
priests 16, 20, 22, 25, 42, 55, 145
primus inter pares 158
priorities 10, 12, 128, 146, 147
proairesis 215, 216
property 99, 124, 127, 168
prophetic role 113
Protestants 77

Q

Qatar 162

R

rapprochement 156, 160, 165, 177, 179, 181
reconciliation 107, 109, 118, 121, 122, 123, 127, 129, 156, 157, 160, 162, 164, 165, 166, 171, 173, 177, 179, 181
refugees 127
Regulations 44, 55, 56
relationship 27, 28, 103, 104, 107, 122, 123, 126, 177, 183, 230
relativization 9, 138, 140, 142, 143
relics 161
religion 38, 49, 80, 85, 93, 97, 98, 102, 125, 126, 163, 164, 165, 174, 179, 183
religious education 48
religious fanaticism 163, 174
religious freedom 56, 73, 118, 125-129
religious minority 162, 168
religious values 89-92, 101
respect 3, 95, 96
Resurrection 20, 79, 106

retired clergy 69
revelation 40, 91, 105, 110, 151
reverence 20, 94-98, 102
righteousness 94, 104, 147
Roman Catholic Church 132, 160, 161
Roman Catholics 77

S

sacred texts 95
sacrifice 100, 106, 221
Saint Basil Academy 2, 29
saints 145
Saints 9, 104
salvation 20, 28, 106, 214, 220
Satan 97
school 13, 15, 21, 42, 46, 63, 64
schools 33, 47, 63, 72, 135, 220
science 34, 47, 164, 165
Scripture 17
secularism 85
secularization 61
security 106, 128
September 11 21, 23, 24, 163
September 11 Relief Fund 24
Sermon on the Mount 104
service 13, 74, 80, 111, 113, 148, 150
Shintoism 92
sin 105, 106, 113, 177, 210, 211, 219
Slavic 134
society 7, 17, 33, 38, 46, 62, 76, 91, 98, 124-128, 145, 146, 162, 213
Society 6, 31, 58, 64, 73, 117, 164
solidarity 120, 126, 127
Sören Kierkegaard 209
souls 23, 79, 82, 90, 104, 106, 219, 221, 223
speech 99, 124, 176

spirituality 41, 104, 107-110, 111-115, 144-147, 152
spiritual retreat 148
Standing Conference of Canonical Orthodox Bishops in the Americas (SCOBA) 2, 25, 30, 57
State Department 56
Stephen the First Martyr 109
stewardship 13
St. Michael's Home 31
St. Nicholas Fund 24
struggle 97, 108, 221, 227
suffering 75, 106, 140
Sunday School 15, 47, 48
SWOT survey 59, 61, 63
symposium 89, 91, 165
synergy 148, 216

T

Taoism 92
Tatian 215
Teachers 8, 104
teaching 9, 15, 41, 47, 62, 63, 66, 72, 109, 150
technology 146
terrorism 38, 115
thankfulness 2, 37, 42
theology 16, 22, 25, 33, 42, 59, 91, 103, 132, 134, 135, 148, 150, 151, 218
Three Hierarchs 132, 211
tolerance 162
tradition 4-10, 12, 15-17, 27, 47, 85, 94-96, 100, 140, 152, 215
traditions 1, 4
tragedy 24, 210
training 11, 15, 57, 62, 65, 170
translations 134, 135, 136, 137
treasures 26, 46, 63, 79

truth 5, 8-11, 15-17, 20, 26, 27, 40, 41, 53, 54, 61-63, 65, 67, 80-82, 84, 105, 109, 110, 113, 114, 117-143, 151, 164, 180-184, 214, 217, 221
Turkey 45, 57, 117, 126, 162, 167, 168, 169, 170
Turkish government 166, 167, 168, 170

U

unchurched 50, 78, 81, 84, 85
United States 45, 73, 74, 77, 81, 126, 136, 152
United States Constitution 126
unity 3, 7, 13, 57, 58, 74, 160, 171

V

values 60, 77, 83, 89-94, 97, 98, 101, 102, 147, 179
vigilance 221
violence 103-106, 108-115
vision 26, 29, 30, 32, 33, 35, 51, 82, 110, 114
visions 10, 35
voice 33, 35, 41, 51, 87, 124, 142, 147, 176, 220

W

wars 38, 213
web site 32
websites 9, 136
wholeness 147, 149-152
wisdom 1, 110, 152, 177, 214, 218
witness 16, 24, 27, 28, 32, 33, 41, 68, 75, 104, 109, 110, 112, 113, 134, 142, 145, 170, 180
witnesses 28

world 5, 7, 9, 13, 16, 17, 19, 20, 25, 26, 32, 33, 38, 41, 45, 53, 55, 61, 68, 87, 89, 90, 92-107, 109, 111-115, 119, 121, 126, 139, 140, 142, 144, 149, 150, 156, 157, 160, 162-167, 171, 173, 177, 180, 209, 218
World Council of Churches 160
worship 1, 4, 5, 10, 11, 12, 17, 27, 40, 41, 59, 98, 114, 118, 120, 121, 123, 125, 129, 138, 144, 148, 150, 152, 182, 220

X

Xenophanes of Colophon 90

Y

YAL (Young Adult League) 30
yin and *yang* 93
young adults 13, 30, 78, 80
youth 30, 43, 78, 83, 175, 225
Youth Department 30